Translated from the French by Jane Brenton
Design and Typesetting: Laurence Maillet
Proofreading: Helen Downey
Colour Separation: IGS, L'Isle d'Espagnac, France
Printed in Portugal by Printer Portuguesa

Originally published in French as *Jardins secrets de Paris*
in 2000 by Flammarion S.A.
Originally published in English as *Secret Gardens of Paris*
in 2000 by Thames & Hudson Inc., and in 2001
by Thames & Hudson Ltd.

This new revised edition simultaneously published in French
as *Jardins secrets de Paris*
© Flammarion, S.A., Paris, 2014

This new revised English-language edition
© Flammarion, S.A., Paris, 2014

ISBN: 978-2-08-020204-8

Dépôt légal: 10/2014

PRIVATE GARDENS OF PARIS

ALEXANDRA D'ARNOUX AND BRUNO DE LAUBADÈRE

Photography by

GILLES DE CHABANEIX

Flammarion

CONTENTS

THE UNKNOWN PARIS

PARIS IS A LEGENDARY CITY, FAMOUS THE WORLD OVER FOR THE BEAUTY OF ITS MONUMENTS, THE RICHES OF ITS MUSEUMS AND THE CREATIVITY OF ITS ARTISTS. IT IS ALSO A CITY IMPREGNATED WITH HISTORY. WALKING AROUND PARIS IS LIKE TRAVELLING THROUGH TIME.

Yet first impressions reflect no more than a part of the city's reality. Behind the magnificent and universally familiar façade, an unknown Paris lies in waiting.

The opulent buildings lining the *grandes avenues* conceal a whole other world, an all but impenetrable secret universe of private gardens. Painstakingly created over the years by their owners or designed by celebrated landscape gardeners, these enclaves of flowers and foliage make Paris a garden city like no other.

Push open the heavy carriage gate, make your way across the magnificent formal courtyard and you will be confronted by a scene from an earlier world, of a striking, spare beauty. The classical gardens of Paris never cease to amaze, with their harmonious proportions, their infinite variations on a standard design, their impassioned quest for equilibrium and cadence.

Alleys of lime, yew and box, clipped square or in spheres, a minimum of flowers – roses and hydrangeas – expanses of verdant lawn:

these are the basic elements that the creator of a classical garden has to play with.

Classical gardens are most often to be found on the *Rive Gauche*, or Left Bank, in the former Faubourg Saint-Germain where in the seventeenth and eighteenth centuries the most elegant private town houses were built. Some of the classical gardens described in the following pages are grand and imposing, others are quite the opposite, with the delightfully contrived simplicity of an Enlightenment folly. Yet others, of smaller dimensions, exhibit the jewel-like charm of the miniature. What all have in common is the highly planned and meticulous appearance that is the mark of the traditional French garden.

However, Parisian gardens are not all in the classical mould, and many other styles of garden feature in the capital's private domain. Rooted in the passions and enthusiasms of their owners, who consciously or unconsciously have attempted to create them in their own image,

the gardens are notable for their imagination, diversity and originality, while reflecting the spirit of the *quartier* they inhabit. Paris is made up of a number of different villages which over time have merged into a whole, without quite losing their separate identities. It is in exploring some of these former villages that you discover gardens in what could be called the 'picturesque' style. Each is a surprise, with its own individual identity. Thus, one particular romantic garden in the 9th arrondissement irresistibly recalls Balzac and his age. There is the last true kitchen garden in the capital, which backs on to the Père-Lachaise cemetery, a reminder that not so very long ago the suburbs of Paris were still green fields. And right in the heart of the Marais is a garden whose friendly, informal air proves that family houses still do exist even in the centre of Paris.

Artists will sometimes turn to the picturesque as a way of maximizing the potential of a restricted space or barren patch of land. These gardens, born of individual inspiration, are always highly distinctive. They appeal to us because they are so richly imaginative, and because we respond to the love of nature and the spirit of conservation that informs them.

Some of the secret gardens of Paris have an alien look. More than simply islands of nature in the heart of the city, they seem to be fragments of a foreign land, transplanted from some fascinating mythological realm. Ever since westerners began to return from their travels with extraordinary descriptions of gardens in the Far East – as well as seeds and cuttings stowed away in their luggage – the taste for exoticism has flourished.

From the eighteenth century onwards, European parks and gardens have benefited richly from the importation of exotic motifs from far-flung corners of the globe. In pre-Revolutionary France, it was fashionable to adorn the most beautiful of the parks on the outskirts of Paris with constructions that illustrated the world's different cultures and civilizations. Among the best known of these are the Tour du Désert de Retz, the Chanteloup pagoda, the Chinese grottoes and the Méréville semaphore. The taste for the exotic is still going strong, and we will end our Parisian tour with a number of gardens that are invitations to distant worlds.

Together, the gardens form a mosaic of open spaces comprising the secret geography of Paris. These plots of greenery tucked away behind the buildings never appear on maps of the capital. Officially, they do not exist. Yet you can sometimes sense their presence – in the spring, for example, when you are walking down a grey street and birdsong suddenly pierces the afternoon air; or when the top of a tree, poking above a wall, is outlined against the sky; or perhaps when a carriage gate swings shut and you glimpse the silhouette of an ancient ivy.

These fleeting impressions offer moments of intense satisfaction to the capital's citizens. It is as if the walls of Paris become briefly transparent, revealing the hidden face of the city. The gardens are oases in a desert of stone, steel and glass. They are a link with the seasons and the untroubled passage of time. A link with a living world.

CLASSICAL
GARDENS

COOL SHADE
AND BRILLIANT LIGHT
designed by Arabella Lennox-Boyd

PARIS'S 7TH ARRONDISSEMENT (AROUND THE EIFFEL TOWER
AND THE MUSÉE D'ORSAY) PROBABLY HAS MORE PRIVATE MANSIONS
WITH GARDENS THAN ANY OTHER AREA OF THE CAPITAL.

Facing page: On the third terrace, tables and chairs are set out beside the statue, whose white marble lightens the shade cast by the tall chestnut trees.

Pages 16–17: Overall view of the garden. The pool and its handsome decorative urn occupy the centre of a lawn bordered with beds of tulips. The goddess on the left seems to smile at the Apollo, hinting at a mysterious complicity.

Today, although it is hard to come by land in this part of the city, it is not totally impossible, with the result that people do sometimes take on barren, sunless plots and proceed, with consummate artistry, to transform them into mini-paradises. As Paul Valéry once wrote, 'as you struggle, so do you think'. When you confront a difficulty, it stimulates the spirit of invention and encourages a complex and intelligent response. Creativity is born of obstacles. Surely the most beautiful garden is the one that was originally a wasteland languishing in darkest shadow, now turned into a shining masterpiece of colour and design?

That is what has happened here. An enclosed plot facing almost due north has been transformed into a garden where the fine spring weather can now be enjoyed in ideal conditions of cool shade and brilliant light. When the present owners first discovered the site, they could not believe that they would ever create a garden out of what was really no more than a gap between two high walls, engulfed in the shade of large chestnut trees. Their decision to take the plunge has been amply rewarded, and the former owner was so thrilled by the metamorphosis that she presented the young couple with a magnificent statue of Apollo to bring them good luck.

The newcomers called on the services of their friend, the English landscape designer Arabella Lennox-Boyd, who decided at the outset to divide the space into three zones. The lower level serves as a terrace extending out from the main living room, providing a delightful spot to eat breakfast in the springtime. Two small flights of steps lead up from here to the second terrace, which is the lightest part of the garden where most of the flowers are planted, and also the area most visible from inside the house. Broad steps

Facing page, top: Festoon
curtains are reflected in the
central pool.

Facing page, bottom:
A profusion of beautifully fresh
'White Triumphator' and
'White Parrot' tulips (left);
a row of boxwood topiary (right).

CLASSICAL GARDENS

then lead on to the top garden, which has two gazebo-like arbours placed symmetrically at either side. From here, the statue of Apollo looks out at an angle, dominating the whole. This is the outdoor dining area, a wonderful spot for suppers and parties.

Once the basic structure was established, Arabella Lennox-Boyd used flowers to complete the transformation. The plane trees were carefully thinned to let in more light and the blank walls covered with trelliswork to support climbing ivy.

The first terrace is decorated with eight camellias in pots and, at the sides, *Agapanthus* 'Albus', *Hedera, Wisteria sinensis* 'Alba', together with *Clematis montana* 'Alexander' and spooneri. 'It is a great delight to look out of the bedroom window in winter and see these camellias in flower', confides the mistress of the house. She and her husband had originally wanted a garden with lots of evergreens rather than flowers, but in the early days of spring both adore the wonderful display that opens with hundreds of white tulips among the greenery, *Tulipa* 'White Triumphator' and *T.* 'White Parrot', followed by *Lilium regale*, all of which bloom in the borders of the second terrace. The steps up to this second area are flanked by clumps of hydrangeas 'Madame Émile Mouillère' and ceanothus 'Blue Mound' in shades of blue and white. Dark blue, blue-grey and white are the dominant colours in this garden, picking up the colours of the façade.

The wonderful equilibrium of the space resides in the interplay of straight lines and curves. On the second terrace, the shape of the small lawn echoes the rectangle of the pool with its flagstone surround, and column-like tree trunks provide vertical straight lines. Softer outlines are supplied by the curves of the clipped box balls and by the domes of the arbours. Two standard hollies flank the steps marking the entrance to the third garden. Their symmetry echoes that of the elegantly proportioned arbours, containing garden chairs and stone benches, which prolong the line of the charming pergola, partially covered in honeysuckle. At the foot of each arch stand tubs of box clipped in spirals, providing an attractive sense of movement against the background of laurels.

On the left, the bust of a goddess seems to smile at the Apollo, reflecting the ever-present happiness in the garden.

CLASSICAL SIMPLICITY
for Hubert de Givenchy

'PARIS IS UNIQUE. YOU NEED TO FLY LOW OVER IT TO GET AN IDEA
OF JUST HOW MANY GARDENS THERE ARE IN THE CITY.'

Facing page, top and bottom left:
The magnificent eighteenth-
century façade and the garden.

Facing page, bottom right:
A seventeenth-century term
from Villarceaux (outside Paris)
stands on the terrace, alongside
pots planted with camellias
and box.

Pages 22–23: Overall view of the
parterres, with the tall trees of
adjoining gardens in
the background.

'Some of them make you gasp with amazement, when you push open
the gates and venture inside', enthuses Hubert de Givenchy, owner of
the Hôtel d'Orrouer in the Faubourg Saint-Germain – once the home
of, among others, the Duc de Montmorency and the Prince de Metternich.
Built in the eighteenth century on the site of former market gardens, the
mansion has retained its original appearance almost unchanged.

Having passed through the porch and crossed the formal courtyard at the
front, you can admire the magnificent proportions of the building and the
classical beauty of the façade with its triangular pediment, a marvel of equilibrium. It is not hard to see why the celebrated fashion designer Hubert de
Givenchy, an art collector with a passion for interior design and a great garden
lover, should have succumbed to this atmosphere of peace and harmony.

The gravelled courtyard is equipped with white planters bearing aloft
clipped spheres of laurel in the manner of torches. Green and white: the
master couturier announces his colours in the front courtyard, setting the
scene for the garden at the rear – in just the same way as the front façade
of the house states the theme echoed in the garden façade.

The steps leading down to the garden at the back of the house are curved,
and flare progressively outwards. On either side of the broad lawn, a path
extends alongside a box-edged parterre where Hubert de Givenchy cultivates
his favourite 'Iceberg' roses. The square-clipped box edging curls round at
each end of the beds to form a rounded clump topped by a dome. That curve
is echoed by the nearby bench. 'I discovered an eighteenth-century model
of a bench, which I had copied because I thought the shape of it matched
the design of the box edging', our host explains. 'When friends are coming,

Facing page: In the foreground,
a bench in the eighteenth-
century style; its rounded forms
echo the shape of the boxwood
hedge that borders the parterre
of 'Iceberg' roses. In the
background, a Medici urn.

we put out green cushions. You don't need much to fill this garden. Person-ally, I don't like places that are cluttered.'

Here there is no necessity for replanting to keep the flowers coming. The roses are still in bloom until the first frosts, and the different varieties of camellia are carefully chosen so that they begin to show at Christmas and continue in flower until September. 'Two *Camellia japonica* "Nobilissima", planted near the house, are the first in flower', Givenchy continues. 'The next in bloom, between the lime trees, is *C. japonica* "Mahotiana Alba", along with *C.* "Madame Charles Biard" and *C. japonica* "Montironi"; the season ends with *C. sasanqua* "Day Dream".' There is the additional advantage with camellias that you can make enchanting little bouquets for interior decoration. This is one of his great pleasures in life.

For Givenchy, profusion often means confusion. His unvarying preference is for classical simplicity, built on foundations of nobility and harmony. 'For me, a garden is first and foremost a place to relax. It should not be a burden. You should be able to say, "My God, I'm longing to sit down, or lie down", and you should be able to do it!' Daily maintenance is taken care of by a single gardener, whose rudimentary equipment – just a pair of secateurs and an old rotary hand mower – is in perfect harmony with the surroundings. And yet the upkeep of such a garden does have its problems. 'Once,' the designer remembers, 'when I wanted to plant some mature trees, they had to be taken right through the house. It was an enchanting and extraordinary sight to see that great mass of roots and branches passing through the salons! A garden is like a house; if you love your house, it will repay you; if you love your garden, it will sense it, and give you back a variety of different sensa-tions, as well as a great deal of pleasure.'

He believes that a garden makes life worth living. 'I benefit from my garden every moment of the day. I love opening my shutters when I wake up, as much when the snow is on the ground as when the birds start singing in springtime. I love the sense that it is alive. Every year and every season, I re-experience the same delights with the same pleasure. I am very happy to have a garden – it is an extraordinary privilege.'

UNDERSTATED ELEGANCE

PARIS REVEALS TO ALL COMERS ITS EXQUISITELY LAID-OUT SQUARES AND AVENUES, AND THE CLASSIC BEAUTY OF ITS MONUMENTS. BUT THERE IS A HIDDEN PARIS TOO, FULL OF UNSUSPECTED TREASURES.

Here, for example, concealed behind the façade of an unexceptional building, lies an eighteenth-century mansion with a courtyard at the front and a garden at the rear. From the courtyard, the fine proportions of the façade are set off by red and white camellias in big planters of classical design. An imposing set of steps under a columned porch leads to the front door. Against the facing wall, a few perfectly trimmed limes hint at a world in which everything is structured, everything planned.

Entering the house, you pass through an antechamber into a large neoclassical salon whose arched French windows open directly on to the garden, as do those in the library and the master bedroom. The south-facing garden had been neglected for years, and was originally little more than a narrowish plot of land sloping down to the boundary wall. The new owner, an interior designer by profession, decided to start from scratch and level the ground. He built a bank extending all along the back wall, intending by means of judicious planting to supply a sense of depth to his new garden.

Facing page: Flanking the steps of the columned porch are two red camellias in planters.

Pages 28–29: The arched French windows of the salon open on to the garden, with a central view of the fountain.

Today, eighty-year-old box balls edge the terrace that extends out from the salon towards the handsome eighteenth-century fountain built on the precise axis of the room.

This feature breaks up the space and encourages the eye to create its own false perspective. To either side of the terrace are two sunken lawns set on a slightly lower level, the route down to them marked by stepped clumps of clipped choisyas terminating in a box ball. At the foot of the steps, smoothly sheared grey-green lavender contrasts with a sprawling mass of day lilies. Adjacent to the wall at the bottom of the garden, the foliage of the lime trees creates a magnificent backdrop. A delightful little building designed by the owner himself occupies one of the corners, serving as a potting shed. Built of freestone and equipped with an œil-de-bœuf window, it could easily date from the eighteenth century.

From the original garden an Irish yew tree, *Taxus hibernica*, was retained, as well as a syringa, now tamed and turned into something quite majestic, almost

Facing page: Globes of clipped box border the terrace. Roses and clematis climb over the wall at the back, offering a contrast with the dark mass of the *Taxus baccata.*

Right: Through the bedroom window, you can see the small outhouse, half-hidden behind a blue ceanothus, and framed by the foliage of the lime trees. To one side grows a clump of bamboo. In the foreground, on the left, stands a *Taxus baccata.*

resembling a maple as it stands by the fountain in an ideal position to catch the rays of the setting sun. A splash of white lilac blossom stands out attractively against the ragged lines of the dark old yew. An apple tree is espaliered against a wall, which it shares with climbing roses – *Rosa* 'Pierre de Ronsard', which is a pinkish white, the white-bloomed *R.* 'City of York', the yellow *R.* 'Mermaid' – and a clematis of a ravishing violet blue. Massed together by the wall are narrow-leaved bamboos, *Arundinaria tesselata.* Everywhere there is this striking contrast between clipped plants and irregular clumps growing in wild profusion. By the bamboo are a small hibiscus and a *Ceanothus arboreus* 'Trewithin Blue', as well as a few hostas selected for their greeny-blue leaves. There is also a shadberry with small white flowers and leaves that turn red in autumn.

To the right of the fountain grows an oleaster, or 'wild olive', *Eleagnus angustifolia*, which has attractive grey-green leaves. A fine holm oak with holly-like leaves, *Quercus ilex*, towers above the area. At its foot are large pots of *Pieris.* The wonderful foliage of *P.* 'Forest Flame' is particularly lovely in early spring. An *Osmanthus*, again with leaves like holly, is paired with a white-flowering *Viburnum carlesii.* In the corner stands a jasmine that bears yellow flowers in winter. Pruned into a low hedge, it serves as a background for rosebushes. Finally, approximately in the middle of the grass, the resident plantsman has put a weeping apple, *Malus* 'Elise Rathke', small and exquisite. Most of the plants came from old family properties, lending the Paris garden an additional nostalgia and charm. At night, lights concealed in the foliage illuminate the fountain, giving the place a fairytale air.

A THEATRICAL STATEMENT

IN A NEIGHBOURHOOD NEAR THE MADELEINE, ON A BEND
IN THE ROAD, AN OLD AND FINELY PROPORTIONED PAVED COURTYARD
GIVES ACCESS TO A PRIVATE MANSION WITH PALLADIAN COLUMNS
DECORATING ITS MAIN FAÇADE.

Facing page, top: The box squares
appear to be a precise extension
of the line of the steps.

Facing page, bottom left:
Louis Benech's landscape
design skilfully contrasts
rigorously geometrical
plantings with the natural
exuberance of the vegetation.

Facing page, bottom right:
The box-edged parterre
is planted with globeflowers
and irises.

When you enter the front door of the house, your eye looks ahead through the hall and is drawn irresistibly out beyond the French windows of the salon to a vast, intricate box-edged parterre, so dramatic that it is as though the curtain has risen on a stage set. Impossible to imagine such a garden, such classical splendour, in a place not already steeped in history. In a previous age, this property was surrounded on all sides by prestigious mansions, the Hôtel d'Arenberg, the Hôtel Suchet and the Hôtel Greffulhe. Each had its garden, connecting with those of its neighbours.

Initially, the present owners had wanted to create an English garden. But the rhododendrons refused to thrive in the shade of the chestnut trees, and it proved difficult to get the lawn established. After three fruitless attempts, they decided on a composition of classical inspiration and to forgo their dreams of green grass. They called in landscape designer Louis Benech, who took as his starting point a recently restored wall clad in trellising. To form a perspective culminating at this wall, he designed an intricately patterned box-edged parterre, enclosed in yew hedges. This gave the garden theatrical impact and a strong identity. 'The only moment the sun penetrates the garden is when it is reflected off the façade of the building opposite', explains Benech, for all the world as if the façade existed only to act as his projector.

As the garden is by no means large, Benech made it look bigger by juggling with the size of the voids enclosed by the box squares. The effect of making these of progressively increasing dimensions is not, as one might expect, to reverse the perspective, but to increase the sense of depth. In this respect, the design is more baroque in inspiration than classical, given that in a classical perspective the voids would need to be of precisely the same size. Another baroque feature is the asymmetry of the two chestnuts, which are slightly out of line. The presence of two silver birches growing at a slant further accentuates the perceived depth of the perspective. The fact that the side path on the left is triangular in form, while that on the right is trapezoidal, once again reflects the typically baroque love of asymmetry. It is because of these irregularities that the garden escapes the severe character of pure classicism and instead has a verve more reminiscent of the Renaissance.

Facing page: An extraordinary effect of perspective is created by the pattern of box squares that terminates at the foot of the wall with its elaborate trellis. On the left, the trunks of the two silver birches seem to mirror one another.

Below: Bordered by a mass of intensely fragrant Mexican orange blossoms, hydrangeas peek out from the shade.

Facing due north and in deep shade, the garden has gained enormously from the new installations, in depth, animation and increased light. The pale gravel lifts the shadows. Where grass refused to grow, the box and yew hedges are now permanently green. The regularity of the central design is tempered by the profusion of wilder-looking plants that form masses at the sides: tufts of white *Iris sibirica*, *Aconitum carmichaelii* 'Arendsii' and *A. napellus*, *Hydrangea* 'Annabelle', *Choisya*, with its delicately perfumed white flowers. The same air of informality is achieved within the box squares by planting such flowers as *Digitalis purpurea* (foxglove), *Japanese anemones* 'Honorine Jobert' and *Boltonia latisquama*. In winter, a superb white camellia is the first to flower. In spring, the chestnuts are in bloom, also white – as are the blossoms of the Mexican orange tree and the hawthorn, whose red berries are such a magnet for the birds. 'The only thing I miss about the English garden,' confides the lady of the house, a nature-lover, 'is that every year the children and I used to collect vast quantities of field mushrooms that grew on the grass, which made wonderful omelettes!' The gravel may not encourage mushrooms, but it is at least planted with bulbs – narcissi and daffodils – which offer a feast for the eyes in springtime.

From the bottom of the garden, it is satisfying to observe how the ornamental steps up to the house are integrated with the box squares, the clean lines of the garden and the architecture subsumed within the overall concept of the design.

Facing page, top: Overlooking the garden is a broad terrace leading off the main reception rooms. The small extension on the left once housed Saint-Simon's study.

Facing page, bottom left: Sunlight pours down on the basement windows flanked by climbing roses.

Facing page, bottom right: An old garden rose.

NATURE HARNESSED
in eighteenth-century style

IN THIS FAMOUS, BUSTLING STREET IN THE 6TH ARRONDISSEMENT
(AROUND THE LATIN QUARTER), IT IS ALMOST IMPOSSIBLE TO BELIEVE THAT,
HIDDEN BEHIND THE ANONYMOUS FAÇADES, THERE IS A GARDEN EXTENDING
FOR WELL OVER AN ACRE, A VERITABLE HAVEN OF PEACE AND DELIGHT
WHERE THE CROWDS AND TRAFFIC SEEM FAR AWAY.

The eighteenth-century house once belonged to the Comte de Saint-Simon, founder of French Socialism, who could look out from his study in an extension at the side of the house, and from there survey the whole garden. We have no idea how the grounds were laid out in his day, but a drawing displayed in the entrance hall shows that in the early years of the twentieth century the garden was designed in the English style.

When the present owners took possession, the land had been neglected for so long that it was little more than a tangle of brushwood. A few fine trees – limes, horse-chestnuts and maples – were the redeeming feature. The owners opted at first for self-sufficiency and started a vegetable garden, before embarking on a total redesign in the French manner. Their first step was to build a large terrace on to the back of the house, looking down over the garden. There is an awning above it, which means you can lunch outside without having to rush indoors at the first drop of rain.

As structural elements, they used yew and box – those fundamentals of the classical garden – and created a leafy bower as a backdrop to the whole. Although the existing trees were magnificent, they had no hesitation in planting more, with the result that twenty-five years later you feel that you are walking in mature parkland. The illusion is fostered by the way the trees

Above: A stone bench
invites contemplation in
the woodland's silence.

Facing page: A majestic
chestnut tree looms above
the garden, casting its shade
over part of the arbour.

are kept neatly pruned, by the high ivy-covered wall and by the row of limes that masks the adjacent buildings.

At the foot of the garden, the thick foliage of tall horse-chestnut trees muffles the sounds of the city. As you stand there, looking back through the shadowy arch of the bower towards the house, you see the white façade bathed in sunlight, apparently far in the distance. In the shade of the flowering horse-chestnuts, where blackbirds shelter from the afternoon heat, an ancient outhouse has survived from the eighteenth century. A path leading to the house passes a bench set in front of old red- and white-flowering rose bushes, splashes of colour against the undergrowth.

Far left: The climbing roses' unrestrained luxuriance almost swallows up a classical head.

Left: Detail of leaves cut from a mahonia shrub in glowing hues of gold and scarlet.

Facing page: A garden path disappears into a mass of rhododendrons.

By the bench, hostas with big pale-green leaves stand out from their mossy carpet. As the heady scent of freshly clipped box mingles with the smells of the undergrowth, and the dappled light filters through the foliage and plays on the grass, you could be a million miles from Paris. Moving on from the bench, you follow a path of old paving stones to the foot of the terrace, where a flight of shallow mossy steps rises between flowering rhododendrons. The walls of the south-facing terrace are covered in glorious climbing roses.

The great charm of this garden lies in its uninterrupted sequence of flowers. In winter, a fine white camellia flowers alongside a glossy-leaved magnolia, and a splendid Spanish jasmine cheers the cold days with its bright yellow. Choisyas and a delicately perfumed white jasmine mark the coming of spring. Daffodils flower on the lawns and an explosion of violets and cyclamen lights up the undergrowth. After that come the rhododendrons and roses. Some of the older roses flower more than once in a season and are still in bloom until late autumn. By then it is time to think about pruning the ivy and box in preparation for the next season.

This garden illustrates a fundamental concept of landscape design in the eighteenth century: everything in it looks completely natural, while nothing is left to chance. Its charm is that of nature harnessed to a purpose.

ROMANCE IN THE AIR

IN 1630, IN THE FAUBOURG SAINT-GERMAIN, A COMMUNITY OF NUNS
UNDER THE PROTECTION OF THE PRINCESSE DE CROÜY FOUNDED
A CONVENT FOR THE DAUGHTERS OF THE NOBILITY.

Above: At the foot of the steps,
by the pretty iron fence,
a mat of baby's tears
(*Helxine soleirolii*) hints at
the presence of water.

So successful was the establishment that the sisters used the accruing revenues to build a number of private mansions. Entering by the magnificent *porte cochère* of one of these houses, you find yourself in a paved courtyard confronting the elegant façade of an eighteenth-century residence. The main salon on the ground floor looks out over a ravishing romantic garden constructed precisely on the axis of the room. Tall French windows open on to a set of steps whose stone balustrades are embellished with tubs of crimson-red heather. At the foot of the steps, a mat of *Helxine soleirolii* (commonly known as 'mind your own business' or 'baby's tears') hints at the presence of water, while a few old white roses flower to one side.

The garden proper consists of a lawn edged with tall trees, among them an American walnut. A massive privet sends out a honeyed perfume when it is in flower. The shade cast by the trees lends the garden a romantic air, accentuated by the presence, at the bottom of the garden, of the music pavilion built by the neoclassical architect Alexandre Brongniart (1739–1813), which is decorated with delightful medallions.

The perimeter is planted with massed shrubs, predominantly choisyas with small scented white flowers, as well as a mahonia, a holly and a large-leaved box. Standing out against this dark background are rose bushes, a hollyhock and a lilac with mauvy-blue blossom. A handsome jasmine grows by the music room. A few clumps of heather in hot colours are scattered below the shrubs, providing splashes of brightness that look like rays of sunshine after showers.

This garden's charm lies in its romantic atmosphere, as well as in a certain sense of nostalgia that is dispelled the moment the sun lights up the façade.

THE MINIATURE GARDEN
of an American in Paris

THE KEY TO THIS SMALL GARDEN IS ITS SIMPLICITY. THE LADY OF THE HOUSE IS AN AMERICAN, A COMMITTED FRANCOPHILE WHO HAS LIVED IN PARIS SINCE SHE MARRIED. SHE CREATED THIS OASIS OF GREEN THAT SERVES AS AN ALL-PURPOSE RETREAT.

'When we moved to the ground floor of this eighteenth-century mansion, instead of a garden, there was just a vile concrete terrace in the shade of a plane tree, and a few box trees. But all around us there were real gardens,' she explains, 'and I just loved gardens too much – their presence, their companionship and the amenity they represent in Paris – not to fall for the idea of planting one of my own to replace that terrace. So I had the concrete taken up and removed, and then I had soil brought in. It was a terrible mess, as the only access was through the apartment! Next came the planting, trying to create the illusion of depth in this confined space. First I hung a trellis on the wall opposite, where I grew ivy. Against this dark background, I placed the large masses of clipped box.'

Planted by the side of a perfect lawn, these box spheres punctuate and animate the space, stating a theme that is picked up by two balls of white stone preserved from the original entrance porch. One is placed at the foot of the clipped box bushes, the other looks as though it has rolled by chance into the lavender border. 'Among the box bushes, I introduced a few shrubs (forsythia, rhododendrons) to provide a contrast. I alternated straight lines with curves, putting a border of clipped lavender along the front of the house, interspersed with bay trees on standards, clipped into spheres.'

Facing page: Above the French windows leading to the garden is a little eighteenth-century balcony. A variety of plants in pots surround the small terrace.

Hydrangeas and a Japanese azalea are planted at the foot of the clipped balls of box that contrast so effectively with the broad-leaved aucubas.

Our hostess now played her trump card, by choosing a restricted palette of colours. Too many, and you destroy the unity of the whole and break up the space. She opted therefore for a symphony of greens, with highlights of white and pink, keeping everything very simple because of the problems of working on such a small canvas. Hence, you move on from the sombre green of the yew near the house to the dark, glossy leaves of the camellia, from the bronze-green of the bay trees to the more subtle shades of the box, from the tender green of the privet to the mottled laurels and the grey-green of the lavender. The touches of white that echo the façade of the house are supplied by the camellia, and then primulas, impatiens and an azalea. Pink highlights are provided by an *Abelia* which flowers from September to November, fragrant pelargoniums and old rose bushes. Yellow rhododendrons and the honeysuckle that sprawls over the hedge provide splashes of brightness in this predominantly shady garden.

'I bring in lots of flowers in pots, lots of rounded shapes, and in that way the space always looks full of plants. With so much going on, it makes my garden look bigger and deeper. The pretty façades all around us seem to protect the garden. They act as a screen for this oasis of green that is such a delight to us, because it makes us aware of the passage of time and the seasons. It's also wonderful to see it in winter, under snow, because the bare bones of the design stand out so cleanly.'

Facing page: A small door
leading to the garden hides in
the shade of the cherry tree.

Below: A catalpa extends
its young branches over
a seventeenth-century bust
of Diana.

ORIGINALITY AND SENSUALITY
on the Île Saint-Louis

THE ÎLE SAINT-LOUIS, AT THE HEART OF HISTORIC PARIS, HAS ALWAYS
HAD A SPECIAL APPEAL. THERE ARE SOME PARTICULARLY FINE
HOUSES ON THE ISLAND, ALTHOUGH FEW WITH GARDENS.
AMONG THE MORE FAMOUS EXAMPLES ARE THE GROUNDS OF
THE HÔTEL LAMBERT, DESIGNED BY THE GREAT SEVENTEENTH-
CENTURY ARCHITECT LOUIS LE VAU.

This, however, is a much less formal garden, installed only recently in the courtyard of a mansion built in 1637 for Jean Le Charron, who was at that time Minister of War. A large entrance porch leads into a superb paved courtyard. Passing on through the main building, you enter a second courtyard which has now been transformed into a garden. Here you are confronted by the building in which the painter Philippe de Champaigne is said to have had his studio, and which was once also occupied by another painter, Ernest Meissonier, in 1840. Today Jacques Bacot, an antiques expert, has converted the ground floor, with its magnificent ceiling restored in the French style, into his office, which is reached through the garden. In 1978, the site was occupied by a cardboard-box factory. 'Luckily the factory went bankrupt! I had it demolished,' he explains, 'then I put down some soil with the idea of making a garden. My first plan was for something in the French style. But, given the setting, I was afraid it would end up looking like a museum piece.' To avoid this trap, something original and a bit experimental was required. Like many impatient amateurs, Bacot wanted his garden to take shape overnight, and he committed the cardinal error of planting privet hedges – known for their rapid growth – and roses chosen for their colour without taking account of the conditions they required. He learned his lesson, and the next time opted

for a more classical design, a touch of originality being provided by the use of yew hedges to line the path leading to the office, creating the effect of a maze. To the right of this path is a large square of grass with an ornamental urn at the centre. Pots of rhododendrons are placed along the pathway that runs beneath a broad terrace with a balustrade.

On the far side, a cherry tree with an intricate pattern of branches marks the way in to the garden. It is a delicious surprise for the visitor, at the right season, to see appetizing red cherries dangling within arm's reach. Another surprise in a similarly rustic vein awaits in the shape of an apple tree trained against a wall, accompanied by a very pretty wisteria. 'This is not a garden to be admired from a distance, it is a garden that takes hold of you physically. It has a strong sensual element: as you pass through it, you can't help stroking the soft shoots of yew and breathing in the scent of freshly mown grass.' Beside the paved pathway, red roses provide splashes of brightness, and a seventeenth-century bust of Diana in white marble offers a contrast with the dark-green yew.

Just in front of the entrance to the office is a low-growing camellia clipped into a square. In flower, it resembles a red 'table' standing on a bed of petals. Near the bust of Diana, Bacot has also planted a catalpa, the foliage of which acts as an attractive sunscreen, and, a little further on, a bay tree in pleasing shades of deep green. Like many another gardener, he rages against the patches of moss that appear on his lawn, the greenfly that play havoc with his roses and, of course, the greed of the blackbirds. In short, Jacques Bacot adores his garden, which serves as an elegant prelude to the handsome interior.

Facing page and above: Allées of yews and rosebushes lead towards the *hôtel's* seventeenth-century façade with its golden-hued stones.

Pages 52–53: View of the garden with a blossoming cherry tree in the foreground.

Below: The awning is inspired by the fabrics of interior decorator Elsie de Woolfe.

Facing page: A delightful spot to sit and relax.

Pages 56–57: A path lined with box hedges leads to one of the garden's sitting areas. Creeping baby's tears (*Helxine soleirolii*) between the flagstones and tall grasses break up the regularity of the design.

A SPIRIT OF ADVENTURE
expressed by Pierre Bergé

'I LOVE GARDENS BECAUSE I LOVE THINGS THAT ARE EPHEMERAL – A GARDEN ISN'T MEANT TO BE A CEMETERY. I HATE CONVENTIONAL, FASHIONABLE GARDENS, I LIKE THEM TO BE ADVENTUROUS,' EXPLAINS PIERRE BERGÉ, DIRECTOR OF THE YVES SAINT LAURENT FASHION EMPIRE, PATRON OF THE ARTS AND GARDEN LOVER.

His eighteenth-century-style house is situated on the Left Bank, a few yards from the Quais. 'I have created an interior that is faithful to its period. As for the garden, it is more French in spirit than in the French style exactly; that is to say, it has a clear structure, but with a certain poetic blurring of the edges.'

When he originally created his garden, Pierre Bergé had no hesitation about starting from scratch, levelling everything to the ground before recreating volumes and depth on the blank canvas that was left. 'To create, you must first destroy. You have to take risks; indeed, that is where the fun lies. To be adventurous is to be alive. You often get it wrong when you're dealing with nature, but when you get it right, it's a great feeling.' It was necessary to remove a handsome tree because it made the place too dark. But people today do not accept that a fine-looking tree may be diseased and dying, and that it needs to be cut down, even if only to be replaced by another. 'At Versailles, it took a catastrophic storm to take out the old wood before replanting could take place', Bergé points out. It is against nature to want to hang on to everything and make it last for ever. 'It's thinking like that that makes people in Paris opt initially for evergreen plants, rather than deciduous. If it's *grandiflora* you want, then by all means go ahead! But, it must be said, it is not absolutely right for the context. Probably they just hate the idea of watching a tree die. Yet in Paris, we exist in a landscape of deciduous trees, destined to follow the seasons, the leaves turning russet in autumn and then disappearing.'

To install his new garden, Bergé chose Pascal Cribier and Louis Benech, both passionate about architecture and plants. 'The restrictions I placed on them? First, no grass! Grass is fine in Normandy. In Paris there is nothing to beat gravel. No lawns, no problems of that sort.' Infinitely preferable are a few grasses and moss growing between the flagstones to give the design a natural appearance. 'And then, I wanted to create different levels, to give an impression of depth.' Bergé also took the decision to lower the sill of the entrance to the house and erect an awning above, so creating a terrace at ground-floor level to serve as an area of transition into the garden. 'I was inspired by what the decorator Elsie de Woolfe had done with fabrics at her house in Versailles.' In the garden, the different levels emphasize the idea of different zones. 'There are steps, and there are the flat-topped box hedges

Left: Detail of a scale-patterned box almost submerged by nasturtiums.

Above, left to right: Beautiful old roses; whimsical sculpture of a trellised cherry tree; the garden in full bloom.

that demarcate the sunken garden where wild flowers are left to self-seed. It all helps to create a sense of movement, and gives me the illusion that I can leave the house and go for a proper walk.'

Many people who bring in landscape gardeners never 'put their oar in', fearing that the plants and flowers will simply keel over and die! Not the case with Pierre Bergé, whose great pleasure is to busy himself in his garden. 'He notices everything, he realizes at once when something isn't working, it was his idea entirely to use topiary,' confides Louis Benech. There is always something new going on. Only recently Bergé had a greenhouse built at the bottom of the garden, to house the orchids he loves to tend.

'I buy plants all the time. As my garden isn't all that big, it's always a question of making a choice, of taking some things out and putting others in. I love grouping plants, anything a bit unusual. People often lack imagination; they don't really make the effort. You see more or less the same thing almost everywhere you go. Choosing plants that are out of the ordinary is more interesting than just copying the garden next door. And I abominate white gardens – they are all the same! To me, they are just proof of an inability to create a garden with colour. White gardens are so sensible. You can be certain you will never get it wrong, and personally I like people who are not afraid to make choices. If they are good choices, all the better, and if they're not, you dig it all up and start again.'

Left: The lively visual poetry of a birdcage and tool shed at the bottom of the garden.

59

A HAVEN OF PEACE
in Saint-Germain-des-Prés

BEHIND THE MUSÉE EUGÈNE DELACROIX, THIS GARDEN IS SITUATED ON
THE VERY SPOT WHERE ONCE STOOD THE VEGETABLE GARDEN BELONGING TO
THE ABBEY OF SAINT-GERMAIN-DES-PRÉS.

Facing page: Four pollarded lime trees form a natural shelter. Box hedges mark the lines of the façade. Visible in the distance is the bell tower of Saint-Germain-des-Prés. Tables and chairs are set out for alfresco dining in spring and summer. This site behind the Musée Eugène Delacroix was once the kitchen garden of the Abbey of Saint-Germain-des-Prés.

When King Philippe Auguste fortified Paris in the twelfth century, the Abbey of Saint-Germain-des-Prés was left outside the city walls, to the south-west of the capital. In those days this was a heavily rural area: instead of broad boulevards and famous cafés, you need to imagine a well-defended monastery with meadows extending along the bank of the Seine. The town engulfed the countryside long ago, and yet, near the old church, a vestige of the past lingers on in the form of a large rectangular garden hidden behind high walls, occupying the site of the orchard of the former Abbey. Dominated now by a seventeenth-century house, this oasis of green is a relic of the ancient meadowland of Saint-Germain that still survives within the modern city.

Everything is neat, natural and timeless: a few white impatiens, easy to maintain, rhododendrons, also white, and neatly pollarded limes. As you explore further, you encounter delicate roses, a hedge of laurels and perfumed choisyas, and ferns planted alongside the walls to provide coolness in summer.

Full of peace and simplicity, this ancient spot has an almost religious feel. Its bareness is in practice the height of luxury, allowing space for the imagination to roam. In the sixteenth century, there must have been pears, apples, peaches and plums growing against the walls, and in the seventeenth century, a splendid vaulted *allée* of hornbeams running on all four sides of the garden. Even more extraordinary would have been the four set-pieces which in the eighteenth century occupied the four corners, intricate arrangements of box and yew that survived until an English garden was installed in the nineteenth century. But surely most beautiful of all is this simple patch of green, where the passing of time is marked by the bells of the church of Saint-Germain-des-Prés.

A LEGACY OF CONTRASTS
from the 1940s

THE PATCHWORK OF GARDENS IN THE 16TH ARRONDISSEMENT,
IN THE WEST OF PARIS, IS A REMINDER OF THE EXTENSIVE PARKLANDS
THAT USED TO GRACE THE CAPITAL BEFORE THEY WERE SWEPT AWAY
IN BARON HAUSSMANN'S WHOLESALE REBUILDING SCHEMES
IN THE NINETEENTH CENTURY.

Facing page: A bed of annuals provides a bright splash of colour at the foot of a bank of vegetation carefully gradated according to height.
The stepped effect creates a sense of depth and makes the nearby building look further away.

Strange to think that today's gardens, huddling behind their screen of apartment blocks, are in many cases the remnants of elegant private estates. The example that concerns us here is attached to a solid 1940s building of somewhat daunting appearance. Here you can be under no illusion but that the city is right on the doorstep. The garden was constructed at the same time as the building, and the boldness of the architecture is matched by the dramatic opposition of straight lines and curves that gives the garden its structure. Well situated, it enjoys sun all day long.

The main reception rooms open on to a wide terrace with an array of low white columns. Looking out from the apartment, you see a large lawn with a profusion of shrubs and trees massed against the boundary walls. The far wall is covered with ivy and honeysuckle supported on trellises, punctuated at intervals by tall maples. This zone of the garden is dominated by curves, with the lawn at the centre and clumps of bushes grouped around it in the English style. The other zone is a complete contrast, with everything based on straight lines. Here there are beds laid out in a chequerboard design and tall, thin trees, notably an old yew clipped to resemble a cypress. This area of the garden is dominated by the first-floor terrace with its balustrade, and squares of trellis on the wall.

The opposition of straight lines and curves provides the garden with a firm architectural framework for the soft floral compositions that change with

Above: At the foot of the
terrace, the chequerboard
parterre is planted with mauve
pansies. It is framed on the left
by a *Taxus baccata* clipped
to resemble a cypress, and
on the right by clumps of
camellias.

Left: A path winds through the
shrubbery, shaded by maples.

Facing page: The bed of pansies
contrasts with the clumps of
choisyas and camellias
in the background.

the seasons. The owner loves to try out new colour schemes and make her garden different every year. This year's dominant theme is mauve, with beds of purple pansies highlighted by red roses, hortensias and rhododendrons. In winter, the garden is white and green: white walls and evergreens like the Caucasus laurel that attractively fills one of the corners without shading the apartment. Beside the wall, in front of the façade, elm trees and a variety of spotted aucubas form a dense mass of foliage, against which are set rhododendrons, camellias and hydrangeas. Behind the shrubs runs a small path lined with hostas, gunneras and skimmias, their long-lasting red berries providing welcome brightness in the shadows. The dense mass of shrubs and cunningly dispersed patches of mauve pansies and white impatiens provide a sense of movement. By breaking up the straight line of the wall, they supply depth to the garden and make it more dynamic. Over to the left, the chequerboard parterre of flagstones is planted with the same mauve pansies and roses. The clipped yew accentuates the vertical.

A young magnolia seems intent on joining the honeysuckle and pots of lavender that decorate the terrace – providing a voluptuous note on which to conclude our visit.

Facing page: The sunny terrace looks out on to a white rhododendron 'Daviesii'. In springtime, the climbing rose 'Albertine' covers the wall with an avalanche of white blooms.

In the background, a *Thuja pyramidalis* sets off the viburnum and rhododendron bushes.

A GARDEN FOR ALL SEASONS

at President and Madame Giscard d'Estaing's home

UNTIL THE 1930S, THE AVENUE DU BOIS – TODAY THE AVENUE FOCH – WAS AT THE HEART OF ONE OF THE MOST ELEGANT *QUARTIERS* IN THE CAPITAL.

Opulent mansions extended from the Étoile (now Place Charles de Gaulle, with the Arc de Triomphe at its centre) to the Porte Dauphine. Fashionable Paris flocked to attend the balls held at the Palais Rose, a replica of the Trianon with walls clad in pink marble, which had been built by Paul-Ernest Sanson in 1896 for Boni de Castellane, while the denizens of high society assembled each morning between the Avenue Malakoff and the Porte Dauphine for their ritual stroll or horse ride.

Of these former glories little remains, but the area is still one of the most pleasant parts of the capital. It is here that former President Giscard d'Estaing and his wife have their Paris home, an attractive mansion with a garden whose apparent simplicity of design conceals a wealth of surprises – combinations of rich and varied foliage and harmonies of colour that reveal themselves only over time. 'When we moved in,' Madame Giscard explains, 'we found an overgrown space with something resembling a lawn hanging on grimly, surrounded by concrete paths. I immediately called in the landscape designer Édouard d'Avdeew, who had already worked with me in the Auvergne, and asked him to invent a garden for all seasons for us.'

It is a garden of contrasts and nuances. A large terrace with a southern aspect extends out from the salon, forming the 'sunny garden', as opposed to the 'shady garden' which is situated on a lower level. The two zones are linked by a flight of steps, flanked on either side by skimmias whose bright-red berries

last the whole year round. 'The high walls covered with trellising – it makes them look less awful – the tall maples and chestnuts, all give an impression of depth,' continues Madame Giscard. 'Because of these verticals, this part of the garden seems much bigger than it is in reality. And that impression is reinforced by the change in level from the terrace above down to the rest of the garden. Different levels confuse the eye, they always have the effect of making a space look bigger.'

The terrace encloses the whole façade. From one end, where the house is set back, a flagstone path extends outwards, edged with thujas, viburnums and rhododendrons. The other, narrower end of the terrace looks down over the shady garden. A few earthenware pots of fragrant geraniums and globes of box form the main decoration, while in the spring the house wall is covered in roses.

The former President's wife loves flowers and plants and has created a garden with a distinctive and elegant style of its own. Thus, the *Thuja pyramidalis* are tapered, like cypresses. At the foot of the first of these, a box ball in a pot provides an attractive contrast, both in shape and in the shade of green. *Pachysandra* is used as ground cover. In spring it is covered with

Pages 68–69: View of the shady garden, with a hundred-year-old mauve-flowering lilac tree in the foreground.

Facing page, left: In the angle of two creeper-covered walls, on a carpet of baby's tears (*Helxine soleirolii*), stands a pink marble basin dating from the seventeenth century.

Facing page, right: Elegant foxgloves tower over the variegated pieris and hellebores.

small white flowers, and the tiny indented leaves harmonize with the intricate, delicate foliage of the geraniums. The calculated contrast of the different greens – grey-green and darker green – is soothing and appealing to the eye.

The larger area of terrace is enclosed by two high walls at right angles. One is occupied by a climbing hydrangea, *Hydrangea petiolaris*, which has dainty white flowers and leaves which in autumn take on a golden hue. The other wall is covered with Virginia creeper, *Ampelopsis*, the foliage of which turns bright red in the late season. A sheared clump of white rhododendrons, *R.* 'Daviesii', stands near the French windows leading to the salon, while in spring the climbing rose 'Albertine' entirely masks the house wall with its avalanche of white blooms. Other rhododendrons and small pots of bergenia follow the sweep of the steps leading down to the shady area. The clear structure we have here, the sense of this being a 'garden of rooms', may not be unconnected with the fact that it previously contained a square-clipped leafy bower, which died because of lack of light. A *Nandina domestica* provides a mass of white flowers next to the steps. The birds love the berries, which resemble mistletoe. Nearby stands a large *Viburnum rhytidophyllum*, quite a rare variety, with wonderfully elegant lanceolate greeny-bronze leaves. Beneath it grow a Portugal laurel and a variegated *Ilex*. 'Pieris, ferns and acanthus flourish here in this patch of shade. I have also extended the lower-level planting with a hawthorn and a *Cercydiphyllum japonicum*, which smells of caramel in autumn.'

Large masses of Portugal laurels, trimmed into spheres, frame the variegated *Buxus*, and provide shelter for the *Ilex, Mahonia*, spotted laurel and hostas that make up the 'undergrowth' – illuminated by a *Hydrangea* 'Annabelle'. The right-hand wall, clad with trellising, is colonized by shade-loving plants such as a *Daphne odora* 'Aureomarginata', a giant acanthus, hellebores, *Hydrangea sargentiana* and *quercifolia*, a *Cornus*, and a *Viburnum wrightii*, a very rare variety with pale-green leaves and wonderful yellow berries. 'I love to feel the way my garden is alive, I love to watch the flowers echoing the seasons,' explains Madame Giscard d'Estaing. 'In my garden, by the time the hostas have disappeared, the hellebores are already out.'

HARMONY AND BALANCE:
An artist's handiwork

AS YOU PUSH OPEN THE CARRIAGE GATES OF THIS HANDSOME
ESTABLISHMENT IN THE 7TH ARRONDISSEMENT, YOU FIND YOURSELF
STANDING IN THE DEEP SHADE OF A LARGE VAULTED ENTRANCE
PORCH. LOOKING A FEW YARDS AHEAD, YOU SEE A PAIR OF IRON
GATES AND BEYOND THEM A GARDEN BATHED IN FULL SUN.

The contrast of light and shade reveals the colours and profusion of the plants in all their glory. A pang of melancholy strikes you, and you are moved to metaphysical speculation on the transience of things. Are shadows a necessary prelude to life's joys? Is the pleasure we derive from our gardens that of experiencing the seasons, of observing the passage of time?

But the house at the rear of this inner courtyard is so bright and welcoming, the garden so delightfully proportioned, that your spirits lift. Clearly, this sense of nostalgia is being deliberately induced; it is a means of enhancing your appreciation of the garden, and making you aware that its ephemeral qualities are bound up with the life of the owner who has charge of it.

Surely, all of us who tend a garden, sometimes for an entire lifetime, do so because we enjoy experiencing through the plants the cycle of the seasons, the way nature alternately slumbers and breaks into life. Gardening exists in total symbiosis with time; it is almost like a manifesto for a particular approach to life. Landscape designer Pascal Cribier understands this perfectly. At the behest of the owner, a cultivated young woman and an artist, he has transformed an unpromising inner courtyard into a garden which, although it looks informal, is actually a small miracle of harmony and balance. Here none of the frenzy of the town has penetrated. In the life of the plants, time flows peacefully by.

Ceanothus branches are trained against the wall and frame the door and windows, the flowers of a delicate mauvy blue emphasizing the proportions of the façade and walkway. Not by chance is this blue the colour that lingers longest on the eye when you are in the shade. The rhythm is picked up in the contrast between the verticals of the trees and the rounded outlines of the box at their feet. Next to the front door stands a fine camellia, covered with a myriad of white flowers in winter. The contrast between light and shade that characterizes this garden is further reinforced by the presence of these glowing white blooms at the darkest time of the year.

Grass grows between the paving stones of the path, an effect both charming and natural, and a reminder that time, far from destroying, becomes a part of things and lends them enchantment. In a small pond near the iron gates stands a white column topped by a stone ball. The branches of an ancient tree are reflected in the surface of the water. All around stand tufts of grass, their pale-green stems and golden heads resembling a fireworks display – a theme taken up by the clipped choisya bushes near the wall when their beautiful little white flowers burst open and release their scent.

Above: Green carpets of baby's tears (*Helxine soleirolii*) are interspersed with paving stones.

SHRUBS AND PERENNIALS:
A harmonious blend

THE RUE BARBET-DE-JOUY IN THE 7TH ARRONDISSEMENT IS LINED
WITH OLD MANSIONS, THE MAJORITY OF WHICH ONCE HAD THEIR OWN
GARDENS. ONE COULD MENTION THE HÔTEL LA ROCHEFOUCAULD-
DOUDEAUVILLE, THE HÔTEL COSTA DE BEAUREGARD, THE HÔTEL
DE SAYVE, THE HÔTEL DE LA TOUR DU PIN-VERCLAUSE, OCCUPIED BY
THE TUNISIAN EMBASSY, THE HÔTEL KOTZOBUE, AND MANY OTHERS.

Just such an *hôtel* was replaced in the 1940s by a house which was fortunate enough to retain the grounds of the original mansion. When the current occupants moved in, armed with the experience of their properties in Normandy and the South of France, they wanted to continue to enjoy the pleasures of a garden in Paris. As the existing one was very old-fashioned, they decided to have it redesigned by landscape designer Christian Fournet.

Originally there was a big terrace of light-coloured flagstones abutting the house and, beyond this, a fair-sized flight of steps leading to an upper level which was simply a gravelled expanse with a plane tree at either end. The steps were centrally positioned on a sloping bank planted with ugly rose trees. The owners wanted to keep the existing arrangement of terrace and steps on the axis of the garden. They wanted a garden in which they could move about easily and which they could look after themselves. 'As I like pruning,' the lady of the house explained, 'I wanted box, laurels and choisyas, but also plants that flowered in the spring and a few evergreens, so as to have a garden that would not be too bare in winter.' On the slopes of the bank, to either side of the steps, Christian Fournet designed box-edged parterres which he planted with new rose bushes. He then used the same design, on a larger scale, for the upper level, filling the beds with an abundance of plants. Against the trellis-clad back wall of the upper terrace, in alignment with the steps, the owners installed a handsome eighteenth-century fountain.

Facing page: Hydrangea *macrophylla* with its white blossoms in full flower.

Below: A clump of *Hydrangea macrophylla* 'Möwe', with flat-headed red and pink flowers.

Above: Side by side in one bed are penstemons, whose straggly stems are a mass of pink flowers in spring, the grey-green foliage and yellowy-green flowers of Euphorbia characias and the white flowers of Rodgersia. Pink peonies complete the picture.

Once redesigned in this simple, classical manner, the garden needed flowers in a restricted palette: white now predominates, with a few touches of yellow and highlights of red. Around the perimeter, Fournet planted camellias, notably a white *Camellia japonica* and a pink *C. sasanqua*; *Cornus*, including a *C. controversa* which has a flat top covered with an expanse of white flowers; *Acer japonicum* 'Aureum' and *A. palmatum* 'Senkaki', with its pretty red wood; also a *Cercidiphyllum*, a shrub with a good shape that provides colour in the autumn. To these he added hydrangeas, *Pieris* and a few yews. On the sloping bank, contained within the box-edged parterres on either side of the steps, Fournet planted white 'Opalia' roses, a variety resistant to the powdery mildew that can be a problem in shady situations. He explains that this choice eliminated the need for complicated treatments. And as an additional bonus, this particular rose is very prolific and allows the owner scope for wonderful flower arrangements in the house. Clipped spheres of bay on standards emphasize the classical theme.

In the two box-edged parterres on the upper terrace, an explosion of plants contrasts with the neatly pruned masses of *Choisya* and a *Viburnum*: growing in joyous profusion are penstemons, euphorbias, white and mauve acanthus, pink peonies and white and red hydrangeas.

At the back of the garden, standing out against the wall, the dark foliage of a venerable *Taxus baccata* supplies a pleasing illusion of depth. A variegated *Ilex aquifolia* 'Albomarginata' relieves the shade cast by the chestnut trees, as do the white panicles of *Sorbaria sorbiflora* with its distinctive leaves. A *Mahonia × media* 'Charity' provides a background for a clump of *Skimmia* and bushes of old roses with crimson blooms.

'Once the garden was redesigned,' Christian Fournet tells us, 'I handed it over to the owner, who looks after it superbly. She is the one who introduces all the changes and keeps it so alive. For my part, I come and visit from time to time, and it's a real delight to see it get better and better as the years go by.'

Left: The eighteenth-century fountain stands at the back of the upper terrace, against a wall that carries an ornamental trellis.

A FINELY TAILORED GARDEN:
Remembering Yves Saint Laurent

YVES SAINT LAURENT ALWAYS HAD A GARDEN, WHETHER IN NORMANDY,
IN MOROCCO, OR AT HIS HOME IN THE 6TH ARRONDISSEMENT IN THE CENTRE OF PARIS.
FOR HIM, COUTURE AND GARDENS SEEMED TO BE ESSENTIAL PARTS OF LIFE –
AND INDEED THE TWO HAVE SOME SIMILARITIES.

Facing page: Tables and chairs provide a focus for informal gatherings on the rectangular white marble terrace, designed by Jean-François Bodin.

A garment is made up of a number of different pieces which need to be assembled, in much the same way as a garden is put together using a variety of plants. Both couturier and gardener are trying all the time to create some sort of unified whole, and they seek to do this by cutting, altering, rearranging and assembling the different elements. Designing a garment with a certain line has something in common with planning the structure of a certain style of garden. Scissors and shears are as essential to the couturier as they are to the gardener. We talk of the 'cut' of a garment, and cutting is an essential skill in tailoring. Equally, every garden has its trees and plants that must be cut back, transplanted, pruned, grafted and propagated by means of cuttings.

Cutting back, taking cuttings, grafting, these all sound like radical measures, but without them the tree would not give such good fruit and plants would never develop new forms and colours. A plant, if it is not pruned, will lose its vigour and good looks, and it is essentially the same with a garment. It too needs to be cut, shaped and adapted. It is painstaking work, demanding close attention to detail while still keeping in mind a vision of the whole – a true feat of creativity. Without it, the garment would be a shapeless piece of fabric, in the same way as a garden without a structure, if it was not kept trimmed and in good shape, would not be a garden.

Facing page: The second
semicircular terrace
dominated by the Minotaur
is equipped with benches of
travertine marble supported
on large globes. The tall trees
create an imposing backdrop.

Right: On the terrace,
a bird chair by
François-Xavier Lalanne.

If elegance in a garment depends on the way it hangs and caresses the body, elegance in a garden depends on a successful combination of plants, the subtle interactions of a restricted range of colours, the linking together of opposites in the form of the verticals and curves that together may be used to set up a rhythm, and the orchestration of different flowers in a harmonious progress through the growing season.

Yves Saint Laurent's Parisian garden, with its strong architectural lines and profusion of foliage (it included several majestic mature trees), represented a blend of disciplined structure and burgeoning growth, an almost perfect illustration of the creative mind at work. A rectangular terrace of white marble, designed by the architect Jean-François Bodin, ran the whole length of the house, matching its sober elegance. The terrace then projected forward in a semicircular extension, its curving outline contrasting with the straight lines of the façade. This curve was echoed by enormous globes used to support benches of travertine marble. The whole was dominated by a fourteenth-century statue of the Minotaur, symbol of humanity in an animal body and perhaps also a metaphor for the marriage of opposites, of the curved and straight line, nature and culture, man and the organic world of plants.

At the behest of Yves Saint Laurent, landscape designer Franz Beachler planted around the terrace, against low trellises, varieties that responded well to pruning: yews, *Taxus baccata* 'Fastigiata', hollies and laurels which, clipped into squares, contrasted strikingly with the unrestrained mass of acacias, sycamores and chestnuts, as airy and imposing as clouds in the sky.

It was a garden designed to make an impact. First there was the shock of seeing on the terrace the two Surrealist chairs in the shape of birds designed by François-Xavier Lalanne, in close proximity to garden chairs made of metal. Then the more gradual realization that the light filtering through the trees created a watery effect of ripples washing over the marble floor. And finally, the sensations aroused by the rustles and scents that emanated from the undergrowth as you strolled along the paths that wind through the trees. All these things gave the place its romantic atmosphere.

The verdict: a garden in the tradition of haute couture that will never go out of fashion.

Facing page: Under a shower of pink blossom, stone steps lead up to a semicircular entrance porch supported on columns and surmounted by a dome.

Pages 86–87: A statue of Bacchus is enthroned beneath the branches of a white horse-chestnut, and flanked by two fan-like *Dicksonia* tree ferns. Behind the statue, the trellis forms a vault, creating the illusion of a kind of grotto.

SYMMETRY AND LUXURY
combined to spectacular effect

ON THE RIGHT BANK THERE ARE A FEW MAGNIFICENT HOUSES WHICH HAVE THE GOOD FORTUNE NOT ONLY TO OVERLOOK ONE OF THE PARKS BUT ALSO TO HAVE GARDENS OF THEIR OWN. THE HOUSE THAT CONCERNS US HERE IS ONE OF THE MOST SUMPTUOUS IN THE WHOLE OF PARIS.

The main entrance is imposing in the extreme, with stone steps leading up to a semicircular porch supported on columns and surmounted by a dome. The wonderfully harmonious proportions of this architectural gem are a feast for the eye. In spring, when the nearby cherry trees are blossoming, it is magical to see the thousands of pink petals strewn over the white stone floor like a carpet. Clipped box balls in tubs line the steps, for all the world as if they have been stationed there to greet you on arrival.

As you pass through the handsome salons, a spacious garden extends before you. All the rooms, indeed, have the advantage of a garden view. The rectangular form is of utter simplicity, and yet it has a stunning impact. It consists of an enormous lawn and a terrace of large flagstones abutting the back of the house. Massed 'Iceberg' roses are planted beside the terrace, in a bed edged with box. Each end of the long rose bed is intersected by a pathway, along which skimmias are placed at intervals, displaying their attractive red berries, accompanied by great globes of clipped box in big eighteenth-century earthenware pots.

Below: Trellised camellias make a spectacular display.

Facing page: In a sheltered corner, beneath a stately *Magnolia grandiflora*, stands a seventeenth-century stone table and its curved bench.

It is this regularity of the layout that gives the garden its rhythm. A small flight of steps leads down to the second level. Immediately facing you is a magnificent Apollo in Carrara marble. In the background, a blue trellis divides the wall into a number of symmetrical panels, providing a sense of depth. A trompe-l'œil niche holds the bust of a Roman emperor, while the pediment above accentuates the classical theme. The wall is covered with magnificent palisaded camellias, a highly unusual way of growing this familiar shrub.

What is so exceptional about camellias is that during the winter, in the dead part of the year, they can be in flower, from Christmas right up to the month of May – something matched by no other species. The effect here is spectacular, with thousands of flowers emerging from the trellis that contains their exuberant display. It is one of the most attractive things in the world to see an abundance of vegetation restrained and tamed in this fashion.

At the end of the camellia-covered wall you come upon a small round terrace forming an island on the carpet of green grass. A stone table with a bulbous foot in the style of Louis XIV, accompanied by a semicircular bench, provides an ideal spot to drink tea and relax while contemplating the sweep of the garden. Right at the back stands a *Magnolia grandiflora* which flowers in summer and sometimes lasts right through till October, providing an admirable foil for the glossy dark-green leaves of the camellias.

The second wall visible from the house is also covered with camellias. At its foot are planted small-leaved bamboos and ferns. Two tall white-flowering chestnuts tower over a Bacchus seated between two *Dicksonia* tree ferns. Behind the statue, a trelliswork arch forms a vault, making it appear that the god occupies some sacred grotto or nymph's retreat.

With its resplendent flowers, this garden is the quintessence of luxury and fecundity. The equilibrium of its proportions and its harmonious colours are evidence of the discrimination and informed taste that went into its making.

PICTURESQUE
GARDENS

NATURE AND SCULPTURE
in a sea of green

THIS GARDEN AT THE BACK OF A PRIVATE MANSION IN
THE 6TH ARRONDISSEMENT HAD BEEN VIRTUALLY ABANDONED
WHEN ITS PRESENT OWNER MOVED IN: ALL THAT SURVIVED
WAS A SINGLE MAGNOLIA ON A SCRAWNY PATCH OF LAWN.

'I didn't particularly want a garden, more a terrace where I could sit in the sun and enjoy some peace and quiet,' she admitted to us. 'But since I have had this garden, I sometimes spend the whole day looking after it! The passion I have developed must come from my father, who used to love gardening. We had a place in Corsica, where I sometimes used to help him. I have also lived in Cornwall, where my in-laws had wonderful gardens.

'There is a park of something like five acres adjoining my house, with ducks, an owl, crows – although I hate their cawing and quarrelling – blackbirds and even goldfinches. The only sounds I hear when I'm at home are the sounds of nature, so every time I go out into the street I feel physically assaulted by the din. I'm very fond of this garden now. I even have butterflies here. And I've enjoyed doing it all myself, with the help of some advice from Louis Benech, who guided me in my choice of plants.

'The first thing I did was bring in more soil and create various levels, so as to have something different from those eternal flat lawns. Changes in the terrain give an effect of depth and leave the imagination free to roam. I then planted not grass but baby's tears (*Helxine soleirolii*), which I think rather resembles cress. Baby's tears has tiny round leaves, it's attractive to look at and it forms a slightly undulating expanse of green that sets you dreaming. To emphasize the sense of movement and create a surface to walk on, I put flagstones down on top of the mossy carpet – they look as if they are just wandering off into the distance, going heaven knows where. In the centre, at the moment, is a big bronze carp, which looks as if it's leaping out of the

Facing page and above:
Two bronze statues stand
on a carpet of baby's tears
(*Helxine soleirolii*): an impressive
male head lends a baroque
atmosphere to this section of
the garden; and a carp,
which seems to be swimming.

93

Below: On the terrace stands
a wrought-iron chair designed
by Madeleine Castaing.

Facing page: From the terrace,
with its border of rose bushes,
a flagstone path leads to
the rest of the garden.
In the background is
an ancient magnolia tree.

waves. The bronze was made by a 1940s sculptor and comes from a collection in Hawaii.

'As for the head lying on the baby's tears (*Helxine soleirolii*), you can't tell if it's a man drowning or just someone swimming in a green sea. That's the only position where I like it. Apparently, at the Château of Versailles, a plan was submitted to Louis XIV – never implemented in fact – for decorating one of the lawns with a number of heads. The carp and the head together do give a faintly surreal effect, especially when my little spaniel Dalila walks in the garden, as they are all just about the same height.

'I took care only to plant species that do well in Paris: azaleas, camellias, old roses. The garden is south-facing, but the trees next door do slightly shade us from the direct sun, which is perfect for the impatiens and the pansies.

'Beside a sixteenth-century basin, in which the birds like to bathe, is a set of garden furniture designed by Madeleine Castaing, which provides an ideal spot for having tea.'

Facing page: The grotto in front of the house is surrounded by shrubs and covered in rock plants.

A RESTORED NINETEENTH-CENTURY GARDEN

THIS ANCIENT STREET IN THE 9TH ARRONDISSEMENT WAS FORMERLY THE ROUTE FROM ROMAN LUTETIA TO THE BUTTE MONTMARTRE. IT IS A PLEASANT SURPRISE TO DISCOVER THAT BEHIND THE TALL FAÇADES OF THE BUILDINGS THE ORIGINAL LARGE GARDENS STILL EXIST, REMINDERS OF A MORE LEISURED WAY OF LIFE THOUGHT TO HAVE VANISHED LONG AGO.

It takes knowledge and skill to preserve this atmosphere of luxurious ease, and that is what makes the garden of this young woman, who is an expert botanist, so very exceptional. 'When I first moved in,' she explains, 'I found an abandoned plot. The trees had been left to their own devices and had taken over completely, there wasn't a square yard which was not in the shade. But the original layout had survived, with a kind of hill at the back and a grotto near the house. It was almost like an imaginary scheme of what a garden was supposed to look like in the nineteenth century.' Firstly, the new owner tried to restore the original design by taking out a few of the trees to let in more light. Both this and the adjacent garden are stocked with the same species, so the clearances in no way detracted from the atmosphere of a shady park that is so typical of the nineteenth century. 'I cleared all around the mound to make it more visible but I left the ground cover of ivy, and at the top I put a table and chairs, hidden behind shrubs. From there, you have a view down over the whole of the garden and the house.'

Below, left: Directly in front of the house stands an *Ilex* which has been pruned to resemble clouds. A profusion of naturalized bulbs grows at its foot.

Below, right: A garden chair stands invitingly in the shade of a tree. Nearby is a large earthenware pot planted with a clipped ball of box.

A path winds around the mound to the top. Growing against the back wall is a Mexican climbing hydrangea, *Hydrangea seemanii*, a plant that tolerates chalky soil and shade, which produces white flowers dotted with pink. At the foot of the mound, to give some structure to the space, the owner installed four square beds, two filled with bushy plants and two, nearer the house, edged with box and planted with low undulating hummocks of baby's tears (*Helxine soleirolii*). The next task was to clear the grotto, which was completely swamped with ivy, now replaced by patches of moss and rock-plants. From the interior of this dark grotto, the garden's exuberant vegetation and wonderful colours look quite miraculous. A table and reclining chairs are set out nearby, close to the foot of the steps with their array of plants in pots. This area functions as a transitional space between house and garden, inside and outside.

Above, left: Poet's jasmine flowers seem to hover over the bench like butterflies.

Above, right: At the foot of a hillock where garden paths intersect, two flower beds are bordered with boxwood.

After restoring the garden's structure, the owner wanted to ensure that it was never without flowers. In January, there are hellebores (*Helleborus orientalis, niger, foetidus* and *corsicus*), *Daphne* and *Sarcococca* – not the more common *S. humilis* but the narrow-leaved *S. querianus*. In springtime, bulbs such as daffodils, irises, scillas and tulips flourish in the sandy soil. For autumn colour, to supplement the fabulous mauve-and-white carpet of cyclamen planted at strategic intervals, *Cotinus obovatus* (the American smoketree), orange with green veins, introduces an unusual note.

'I love daphnes,' confides the owner, 'especially *Daphne odora* "Aureomarginata", because there is nothing more amazing in the depth of winter than going out into your icy garden to see these little pink, red and white flowers that smell so marvellous. In summer I grow white and pink *Phlomis*. It's a rather wild-looking plant, the colours of which go very well with the dark green of the garden. And then I have my favourite small trees – some of the maples, for example. There's one here, *Acer oblongum*, which is grown from a seedling I picked up at the Serres de la Madone in the South of France. It's one of those rare evergreen maples. I also like the white-flowered *Osmantus armatus*, which grows intertwined with *Clematis armandi*, and the arbutuses, particularly *Arbutus × andrachnoides*, which has a lovely cinnamon-coloured bark. And there's a buddleia I'm fond of, because its fragrant flowers come out in September and October, attracting hordes of butterflies, just at the time I return to Paris after the summer.'

Facing page: Large shrubs in pots accompany the wooden reclining chairs set out beside the house.

There are a lot of ceanothus shrubs, because they stand up well to the Parisian climate, flower twice a year and form dense clumps, as well as a hedge, of a ravishing blue. Then some interesting *Cornus* varieties, with their twisted leaves – notably a *C. sanguinea*, chosen for its coloured wood, and *C. alba* 'Aurea', which brightens dark corners with its yellow foliage. As you explore further, you come across holly and privets, including a Chinese variety, which has long bamboo-like leaves, a *Mahonia cumula*, which grows particularly well in Paris, a *Viburnum odoratissimum* with exceptionally attractive foliage and a *Magnolia grandiflora* 'Little Gem'. The owner also had fun building up her small collection of Californian evergreen oaks, which bear long, narrow leaves. Among the rarer plants is an *Aucuba* 'Longifolia', covered in winter with round red berries.

'A garden,' she insists, 'is an ensemble that only works if you continually pay attention to every last detail. It's a living thing: on the one hand, you have to prune, clear out the dead wood, and on the other, you have to allow things to grow. A garden is a world of its own: the seeds are brought in by the birds, you cut the flowers to make bouquets, the herbs are for the kitchen. I like to walk around it and inspect my plants, clip the box and the hedges. There are structural areas which shouldn't change, and others you dedicate to planting new things. One plant won't do anything in one particular spot, but grows perfectly well a yard away. There is an equation that has to be balanced between choice of species, number of plants and favourable situation. It is all so wonderfully alive and brings such real pleasure.'

RESTRAINED LUXURIANCE
designed by Camille Muller

IN THE 13TH ARRONDISSEMENT (IN THE SOUTH-EAST OF THE CITY)
THERE ARE STILL A FEW LUCKY SOULS WHO LIVE IN HOUSES
SET IN THEIR OWN GROUNDS.

Facing page: A wooden bench
in a shady corner of the garden
provides an enticing spot
to while away the time.

Pages 104–5: A view of
the house through the trees.

Just off a rather dour street running alongside La Santé prison is a discreet cul-de-sac with low, well-proportioned houses on either side. A wonderfully provincial air prevails. Some of the houses look as if they might belong to someone famous, with their large, tree-filled gardens; others are more modest, but still highly desirable. What once was countryside is now reduced to pockets of green left untouched by the urban sprawl.

The house that concerns us is at the far end of the cul-de-sac, tucked away behind a low wall covered with ivy and honeysuckle, from which a few straggling roses emerge. You enter the garden by what looks like a secret door, and as you penetrate the curtain of foliage Paris feels a million miles away. And yet for a long time this garden was fallow land, without much in the way of plants, only a few trees. It so happened that one day the owner was trying to find out about plants that would tolerate shade, and by pure chance she met the landscape designer Camille Muller. He specializes in overcoming the problems of heavy shade, and agreed to take charge of installing a new garden. The work would take a year.

Muller decided to make a virtue of the various constraints. The low wall that divided the garden was redesigned as a series of curves, creating a number of different levels. The shade that made the lawn such an unattractive feature gave him the idea of putting down old paving stones and patches of gravel to lighten up the area. The garden was given a 'skeleton' of plants tolerant of half-shade. The owners hated the idea of anything that was too precisely planned; they wanted something that looked natural, was pleasant to be in, green in winter and cool in summer, with moss growing on the paving stones. Taking his cue from them, Muller planted bamboo on the road

side of the house, to give greater privacy and reinforce the impression of luxuriance and depth. He massed plants together in groups, with paved paths running between them that led to gravelled areas. This provided a coherent and attractive overall scheme. Framing and containing the luxuriant foliage in this way works particularly well. There is not a single spot where the eye is not drawn on towards a vanishing point, a clearing or a pathway leading into the distance.

The massed bushes are sometimes punctuated by spheres of clipped box, which temper the wild abundance of the vegetation. In appearance a jungle, the garden is in fact made up of a number of different but complementary spaces. Almost lost in greenery is a bench that offers a pleasant respite. Near the house, an old rope hammock is suspended between two trees, to the vast delight of the children who chatter away in it like birds in a nest. A table and chairs are set out under the spreading branches of an apricot tree. As soon as the first fine days of spring arrive, the family enjoy their lunch there, sometimes lingering long after the meal is over. In late afternoon, a ray of sunlight picks out the pretty fountain half-hidden behind a clump of bamboo and ferns. The area of old paving stones outside the back door provides a focus for the plants massed around the house, giving it a slightly old-world appearance. Climbing roses festoon the doorway and a small acacia has self-seeded right in the middle of the path. There are fruit trees that are a delight to all: a cherry regularly plundered by the blackbirds, a prolific walnut which produces basketfuls of nuts in the autumn, and best of all the apricot, which every second year in mid-July produces an abundance of excellent fruit.

Apart from the roses there are very few flowers. But the acanthuses do well, as does the *Hydrangea arborescens* 'Annabelle' and the treelike *H. quercifolia*, whose evergreen leaves turn red in the autumn. To give 'bones' to all this luxuriant growth, Camille Muller has used evergreens such as *Nandina domestica*, *Mahonia*, holly and Portugal laurels. Set off by its new garden, the house is quite transformed.

MEMORIES OF BRITTANY
on the Montagne Sainte-Geneviève

THE *QUARTIER* OF THE MONTAGNE SAINTE-GENEVIÈVE, THE HILL
ON WHICH THE PANTHÉON STANDS, IS ONE OF THE OLDEST IN
PARIS AND STILL RELATIVELY UNSPOILT. EVEN TODAY THE PLACE DE
LA CONTRESCARPE RETAINS MUCH OF ITS VILLAGE ATMOSPHERE.

Facing page: Details of this
vibrant, picturesque garden.

Only a stone's throw from the square, where the Rue Mouffetard begins, an antique-dealer couple, Pierre and Dominique Benar-Despalle, have set up in business. They were not interested in a conventional shop that opened directly on to the street, preferring to think that being a little off the beaten track would make the pleasure of discovery all the sweeter.

After passing through the main entrance and then a pair of iron gates, you walk down a narrow passageway, the walls of which are covered in roses in the springtime. You arrive at the first small garden, and a building that is a cross between a house and a loft. Here, removed from the bustle of the city, Pierre and Dominique entertain their clients every Thursday, as if they were long-lost friends. In these relaxed surroundings, the furniture and objets d'art retain all their original charm. A second small garden at the back of the building provides access to the workshop and the house.

'When we decided to move in,' Dominique explains, 'there were workshops here making copperplates for engravers. Creating the gardens was a titanic struggle. The buildings had to be demolished and the concrete floors broken up, and then the soil had to be wheeled in in barrows along that narrow passageway! I was brought up in the country and I can't do without nature. I can live in a small house, but I do need a garden. Nature reminds me of the happy childhood I had. The soil is linked to the seasons: winter passing, spring returning. If you fight against it, that's cheating. That's the truth of nature. Its freshness and purity give you an equilibrium. For me, all the beauties of the world are contained within my garden. It's a very humble

one and I maintain it on my own. My garden is a living thing; what I mean by that is that it's not always looked after. I can let a year go by without doing anything to it – there are times when it just lies fallow, then there are other times when it's awesome.

'It's also a place I walk about in. I never relax in a deckchair. I'd rather perch on a stone, write, sketch, dream. For me, this garden is not a hobby, it's a way of life, a philosophy for living. I'm always moving my plants and replacing them. There are pear and apple trees and a vine which produces huge bunches of chasselas grapes. You meet a lot of creatures in my garden: birds that come and take a dust-bath on the stones, the tortoise that disappears for ages and then turns up again. I have lots of little succulents in pots that I bring back from wherever I've been. Some of them make me think of Bonnard or Matisse. Plants have such a strong presence. There's one that comes from Venice, which fell off a balcony. I also have stones I like which come from Brittany, where I used to live with my father, who was a great nature lover. He was a pharmacist and also a herbalist, and when we went for walks he used to recite all the Latin names of the plants. There's a piece

Facing page: Framed by
climbing wisteria,
pots of succulents are
set out on a table.

Below: Old watering can
and pots of succulents.

of Breton granite covered in lichen; it's like having a little Breton chapel in my back garden. This garden contains scraps of my history. It's as graphic as a poem. Everybody gets something out of it. My husband does the pruning, my daughter just hangs out.

'In the morning I get up very early and wander round the garden with my cup of coffee, a bit like a peasant in the big city. At night when I can't sleep I go out in the garden. It's astonishing, nothing looks grey; what you see are greens, yellows and ochres. The night has one particular colour, a sort of golden haze. It's beautiful because it's so muted. In the morning, the first thing I do is look at the sky, to see whether it's raining or sunny, to look at the clarity of the light. A garden is paradise on earth. I don't need to go away. Everything is here, if you know how to look. You can watch the flowers growing. The roses are like an avalanche in May, then they come back in July, and some come again even in December.

'Every year my white wisteria is a delight. I pick fruit: pears, apples and currants. I clip the box. Box helps as part of the design when it's clipped in the shape of a ball. For me, box means permanent green, it means Italy. There are all sorts: round-leaved, pointed, variegated. I take my cuttings, I watch over them, I prick them out. The more I do it, the more I have a fancy for a real parish priest's garden. I dig, and I feel healthily tired. I enjoy each season. Each has its rhythms, its different qualities and images. When I return home in August, the garden is lush, a riot of growth. I leave the weeds that have appeared while I was away until the big winter clear-up. Most of all I love the winter, its harshness, that bare look, the damp. People think it's a dead season, but it's really a long sleep while everything recovers its strength. When the plants are pruned, there is a kind of bleakness, but you sense a great power lurking there. Spring is wonderful, of course, all freshness and tender green shoots, but I don't like summer that much. In the autumn, on the other hand, when the trees shed their leaves, you have the pleasure of trampling them underfoot. Nature gives us an extraordinary lesson in life; everything is always being renewed. It's a cause for nostalgia, but also for joy.'

AN UNUSUAL
KITCHEN GARDEN

THE EXTRAORDINARY THING ABOUT MISHKA'S KITCHEN GARDEN –
APART FROM THE FACT THAT FLOWERS AND VEGETABLES
ARE GROWING HAPPILY TOGETHER IN THE HEART OF THE
20TH ARRONDISSEMENT, IN THE EAST OF THE CITY – IS THAT IT
BACKS ON TO PÈRE-LACHAISE, THE CAPITAL'S BIGGEST CEMETERY.

All that separates the hundred or so acres of Père-Lachaise from one of the last vegetable gardens in Paris is an old wall with a trellis on top, beside which stand a water-butt and some ancient watering cans. Mishka's garden is a sort of urban miracle. It is a well-kept secret, a rural retreat hidden away behind a twentieth-century apartment block that in turn masks an elegant eighteenth-century folly, which would once have possessed a fine park of its own. Now that only this island of vegetation remains between the buildings, it feels like an uncharted wilderness.

Access to Mishka's kitchen garden is via a path that threads its way through a patchwork of small gardens left largely to their own devices. The grass is so tall that it is like cutting a path through a meadow. There are scattered poppies and tufts of larkspur growing to head height. You notice in passing a bamboo cane laid on the ground to mark the boundary of a freshly cleared plot.

'I can't live without a garden', Mishka explains. 'I spent my childhood at Les Essarts just outside Paris where there was a marvellous garden, and that gave me my love of nature. Then I lived for a long while in the west of Canada with my husband, who is a writer and as much in love with plants and travelling as I am. We had a garden over there. So it seemed quite natural to me, when we got back, to have one in Paris so that we would still have a sense of the passing seasons, some contact with the soil. Ten years ago, I was lucky enough to be able to buy this plot and prevent it being taken over for housing.'

Facing page, top:
A wooden water-butt and
two old watering cans
stand by the wall.

Facing page, bottom:
A folding table and chairs are
set out in a shady spot under
a horse-chestnut tree.

Here there are no grids, no master plans, no regimented rows of vegetables. On the contrary, everything seems to grow with total freedom. As you pass under an arch thick with the grey-green foliage of an oleaster, you come upon a wooden cabin at the far end of the garden, in the shade of a splendid chestnut tree with irises clustered at its foot. This is where Mishka comes when she feels like visiting her flowers, doing some planting or hoeing or simply having a stroll. Sometimes she makes tea out of doors in an ancient little iron kettle, which stands on bricks to heat up over a makeshift fire. The cabin is right next to the wall of the cemetery, and the many tall trees that grow there create the impression of spacious and peaceful parkland. You cannot help but think of Jean-Jacques Rousseau's small hut in the depths of the country, his dreams of the life of the noble savage.

'Sometimes I desert the garden for a long time, at others I'm here every day. I love this place. It took me months to clear and I intend to keep it up. This is a world in miniature. It's my way of doing something for the planet, my way of returning it to its virgin state.'

An old vine growing on the wall was replaced with new stocks from which Mishka makes a delicious Hamburg Muscat. In an old wooden tub, 'the very same one we used for the horses to drink from when I was a child', she collects rainwater for her plants. A little further on she has put a fig tree which produces a delicious crop of white Argenteuil figs. The garden also has an apple tree, two espaliered pears and even a bush peach. At first sight it looks as if nothing would ever grow in this tangle of vegetation, yet everything seems to flourish, whether flowers, vegetables or fruit. Kiwi vines climb all over the wall. There are blackcurrant, a raspberry and some gooseberry bushes, reminders of the abundant vegetable gardens and orchards of the past.

Left: A virtual ballet of
zucchini blossoms.

Page 113 and facing page:
The lush abundance of
the garden contrasts
with the nearby buildings.

Mishka is fond of climbing plants: jasmine, clematis, bignonia, honeysuckle –
even the roses you see clambering among the trees. She adores the scent of
syringa and the fragrance of that fine old rose variety, 'Cuisse de Nymphe'.
'I love hollyhocks growing out of tall grass. They go very well with acanthus,
those wonderful artichoke flowers, and honesty.' As for trees, you come across
hazels, an elderberry (some of whose purple berries Mishka uses for jam), and
a white-flowered shadberry, planted as a souvenir of Canada, where the bears
love to eat the fruit. Sometimes Mishka makes piles of twigs, so that the insects
that thrive among them will prove an irresistible attraction to the birds. She
also grows borage, which the bees adore. Her intention is to achieve a balance
between insects, birds and flora. The manure she uses is a combination of
ashes, liquefied nettles and a decoction of horsetail. But most astonishing of
all are the vegetable beds. Although overshadowed by the luxuriant vegetation
on all sides, these tiny plots are miracles of perfection. Here are the carefully
nurtured beds of seedlings, fresh as can be and still totally vulnerable, as well
as Portuguese cabbage, onions, broad beans and rocket. It looks more like a
doll's tea party set out by a child, not really meant for eating. To one side is
the herb garden, with thyme, tarragon, chervil, coriander, wormwood and mint.
Here, where everything grows higgledy-piggledy – globes of box amid the tall
grass, vegetables mixed in with roses – Mishka feels at home. She knows there
are wild rabbits and even a dormouse, and it is her dearest wish to come face
to face with a hedgehog.

Facing page: The house
and garden, in the shade of
a splendid acacia.

A NINETEENTH-CENTURY ACTOR'S SANCTUARY

QUITE A FEW ARTISTS HAVE BEEN ATTRACTED TO THE
9TH ARRONDISSEMENT. AUGUSTE RENOIR AND VICTOR HUGO
WERE LONG-TIME RESIDENTS, AND GUSTAVE MOREAU
HAD BOTH HIS HOUSE AND HIS STUDIO THERE.

But long before that, back in the days of the First Empire (1804–15), people used to flock up the hill rising above what is now the church of La Trinité to attend the performances of the celebrated François-Joseph Talma, Napoleon's favourite tragedian. Adjacent to Talma's theatre was his house, and one can imagine that his private and professional worlds were closely linked – although not perhaps to quite the same degree as the Emperor's who, when he was at Malmaison, was so desperate not to waste a single second that he would slide down a spiral staircase leading directly from his bedside to his office!

When Talma left the theatre, he could return home through the garden, which in those days was filled with classical statues. When the present owner moved in, the garden possessed nothing of its former glory and had largely reverted to virgin forest. But near the house was a large *Buxus* that had reached the size of a tree, which he realized must be well over a century old. It was the box tree that made him decide to buy the house. 'I have always lived in houses with gardens, and I realize now that I only like living on the ground floor, because there you are directly in contact with the earth.'

Facing page, top left:
A two-hundred-year-old box
tree shelters a drift of pink and
white impatiens bordered
with lavender.

Facing page, top right: Ivy
encroaches on a bonsai tree
beside a bed of camellias.

Facing page, bottom left:
A garden table and chairs are
set out on the wooden decking
that extends out from the
terrace, making this an ideal
spot for breakfast in the cool
of the early morning, or for
quietly reading a book in
the evening shade.

The house is in the Directoire style, with a white façade punctuated by louvred shutters. The salon occupies a semicircular area projecting out from the centre of the façade, with an array of French windows opening on to the garden. From inside the room, you look out over a fine English-style lawn with a number of large trees, notably an acacia whose delicate foliage trembles in the slightest breeze and a magnificent magnolia which flowers in spring. Beneath the box tree, currently pruned in an attractive dome shape, lavender bushes border a drift of pink and white impatiens. The massed shrubs surrounding the lawn are varieties of hydrangea, among them the superbly elegant *Hydrangea serrata* 'Grayswood', which has flat leaves, and the classic fast-growing variety *H.* 'Madame Émile Mouillère', whose ivory-white flowers look particularly ravishing in combination with fragrant old roses.

At the far end of the garden, from a bench placed beside sweet-smelling choisya bushes, you can enjoy the prospect of the house and all its grounds. To one side is a remarkable bonsai tree, whose simplified lines add a contemporary touch.

'Because of my windows, I always feel I am already in my garden when I wake up. There's a little ritual, when I go out in my dressing-gown with my cup of coffee. Of course, there are times when I neglect my garden because of lack of time, and I never have enough chance to enjoy it, but I can't live without it. It is a part of me. It is actually more important to me than the apartment.'

AN INFORMAL FAMILY GARDEN
in the Marais

THE *QUARTIER* OF PARIS CALLED THE MARAIS, ON THE RIGHT BANK,
IN THE HEART OF THE CITY, DERIVES ITS NAME FROM THE MARSHLAND
OF WHICH IT USED TO CONSIST BEFORE BEING DRAINED AND RECLAIMED
BY RELIGIOUS COMMUNITIES IN THE THIRTEENTH CENTURY. BY THE SIXTEENTH
AND SEVENTEENTH CENTURIES, THE MARAIS HAD BECOME ONE OF
THE MOST FASHIONABLE AREAS OF PARIS, WITH MORE PRIVATELY OWNED
MANSIONS THAN ANYWHERE ELSE.

Facing page: The magnolia tree, with a bed of white impatiens nearby.

In the nineteenth century, as the result of the reorganization carried out by Baron Haussmann in his mission to clear away the maze of medieval lanes, the area entered a long period of decline. It is only in the last twenty years that major renovations have begun. The garden that is the object of our visit belongs to the first wave of these refurbishments. 'At that time,' the mistress of the house explains, 'it seemed rather a risk to buy a whole house, in the Marais, and one with a garden at that. I had just got married and we were regarded as pretty odd to move away from the Place Victor-Hugo! If, instead of buying this big house and garden, we had bought a flat in the 16th arrondissement, we certainly wouldn't have had five children.' A true home, the property has adapted over the years to the needs of a growing family.

'It is a Renaissance house, and at the time we bought it, it was in a terrible state. The garden had been used as a dump, and then it was partly dug up when an underground car park was put in. It was a tip. But we took the gamble. By a curious combination of events, at just about the same time we had to take responsibility for a listed property belonging to the family, and we became aware of how different the problems are – you can't approach the restoration of a country estate in the same way as you would tackle a Paris garden. I didn't have any particular enthusiasm for the subject originally, but

Above: From the balcony,
you look down on the plants
that came as gifts to the owner
from her friends.

it was the king's vegetable gardens at Versailles and the formal beds of the Jardin du Luxembourg that awakened my interest, and taught me what I know.'

The young couple embarked on a major programme of works at their new Paris home, completely refitting the whole house, importing tons of soil to fill in the gaping hole and transplanting a mature magnolia. 'Things got done gradually, with the help of two students from the School of Landscape Design. Of all garden tools, the magic wand is the worst, and patience the greatest virtue.'

The garden is situated at a lower level than the house, and you go down to it via a flight of steps broken by a landing. From here you can survey the lawn shaded by the magnolia, which established itself wonderfully, and the silver birches. There is the usual garden shed, standing next to a big bay tree, and a corner with a table and chairs. The choice of plants is sometimes a little surprising, as they largely consist of gifts presented by friends. The whole thing has an informal air rare in Parisian gardens, especially in this historic quarter. 'I grouped together at the foot of the steps what I call the "thank-yous". There are a lot of mop-head hortensias, which I am trying gradually to replace with more interesting kinds of hydrangea. And at one point I was practically overrun with pittosporums. The lawn, on the other

Below, left: An attractive combination of white blooms, with the off-white flower-heads of hydrangeas paired with pure-white impatiens.

Below, right: Furnished with a table and chairs and a variety of plants in earthenware pots, the sitting area offers a pleasant view of the garden.

hand, never really did anything because the garden is too shady. I replaced it with baby's tears (*Helxine soleirolii*), which was a complete success, and I added some roots of acanthus. I love the heavily cut, curving shape of the long, wonderfully ornamental leaves. I even have a fig which grew from a branch that was just thrown away without a second thought, and which to our surprise began to sprout.'

This young woman who used to take no interest in gardens now spends long hours pruning, sowing and pricking out. 'In a way it's my laboratory. I take cuttings from the raspberries in the country, I stick them in the ground and it just seems to work. I have made every mistake it's possible to make, and now I don't go too badly wrong. Learning on the job seems to me an excellent philosophy. I like most things, with the exception of anything tropical – too fragile and brightly coloured under Parisian skies. The thing I like most about the garden is that each element reminds me of someone or something.'

A FEMININE AMBIENCE
inspired by fashion and art

A TALENTED PAINTER AND FASHION DESIGNER, ANNE-MARIE BERETTA
MATCHES HER ENTHUSIASM FOR FASHION AND ART WITH A REAL
PASSION FOR GARDENS. MOST OF ALL SHE LOVES THE WAY COLOURS
AND SHAPES ARE CONSTANTLY CHANGING AND ASSUMING NEW
PATTERNS.

When you enter her apartment through the tall French windows that link it to the garden, you are struck at once by the animation and colour of the decorative scheme. Clearly her eclectic creativity inspires her interiors as well as her garden.

When winter comes, Anne-Marie brings indoors a number of the plants, among them the two magnificent lemon trees in big pots from Anduze (in the Cévennes region of the South of France), as well as her mandarin orange trees and variegated begonias; and she also brings in the birds that she keeps in a spacious cage. Throughout the winter, her apartment virtually becomes a garden. She takes just as much care of her outdoor plants as she does of her birds. In 1986, when there was a very severe winter and a hard frost, she covered up the plants with anything that came to hand and catastrophe was averted.

Landscape artist Camille Muller designed the overall plan for the garden, but it was Anne-Marie Beretta who wrought the transformation, bit by bit. 'It's a real delight to come back here and see all the wonderful things she keeps putting in her garden', Muller comments. Anne-Marie plants things that interest her, grows trees from fruit stones, moves things around, prunes, keeps an eye on everything and generally brings the garden to life. In the sense that she has an empathetic relationship with everything here, you would be justified in describing this as a feminine garden.

Facing south, the garden extends outwards from a terrace lined with Anduze pots planted with lemon trees, globes of box, lavender and even a

Facing page: All the plants and trees growing in the garden seem to be spilling out of the gigantic shell in the foreground.

small palm. Growing among the roses on the façade is an espaliered pear tree. The lawn beyond the house is edged with bushes and trees that form a mass of layered vegetation, with patches of dense foliage cunningly contrived to suggest depth. From her former garden Anne-Marie brought with her a polygonum that is now over twenty years old. Every year, when it is covered with white flowers, it acts as a magnet for the birds of the Bois de Boulogne (the large park in the west of the city): 'There are robins, tits, bullfinches, goldcrests, and, of course, blackbirds.' The giant Anduze pots to the right and left of the terrace help to give a sense of scale to this quite small plot. Anne-Marie Beretta has used them to plant mandarin orange trees and peonies with silky pink and white petals. She adores fruit trees and, as well as the espaliered pear, which is covered in lovely pale-green leaves in early spring, there are also apple trees with sumptuous blossom, a Japanese medlar (or Japanese plum) and a peach tree that is sometimes so laden with fruit she has to use it for jam. 'The method of propagation is quite simple. I put the fruit stones in pots, which are protected with mesh from the birds, and when they break open, I replant them. After that, all you need is a lot of patience.' She also grows a number of other trees rarely found in Parisian gardens: a sorb, a few spindle trees, a mahonia, also a *Phillyrea angustifolia*, a *Deutzia* (a handsome bush with white flowers), and a *Vitex* with elongated leaves, blue flowers and a camphor-like perfume. She has also planted white camellias with a yellow centre, *Camellia japonica* and *C. sasanqua* 'Papaver', which has fragrant flowers, one of the few camellias to have any scent.

Originally, Anne-Marie Beretta dreamed of a white garden. However, she quickly came to the conclusion that her natural preference was actually for something brighter, and chose orange as the main colour for her roses. And as pale yellow is a very pretty shade to brighten up dark corners, she opted for *Rosa* 'Mermaid'. The various different greens are delightful, ranging from the deep green of the camellias, box and laurel to the light green of the fruit trees and grey-green of the olive. The foliage is of all kinds and shapes: short, rounded leaves for the camellias, elongated ovals for the azaleas, lanceolate for the bamboo and olive. The garden has a favourable aspect and good light. The presence of birds, fruit and flowers all together makes it feel very much alive, and the discriminating choice of plant species lends it additional charm.

Facing page, top left: A window and its balcony are immersed in luxuriant foliage.

Facing page, top right: One of Anne-Marie Beretta's favourite orange roses.

Facing page, bottom left: Two deckchairs are installed against a rose-covered wall between a sphere of box and a pair of lemon trees in pots.

Facing page, bottom right: Tall roses blossom among the pale-green leaves of a peach tree, grown from the stone of a fruit by Anne-Marie.

Facing page: The pink-and-white flowers of clematis 'Nelly Moser' cover the wall and the stone bust mounted on a stele.

Page 132: An ornamental column next to the wall is framed by a cascade of red roses.

Page 133: The oval pond in the centre is set away from the wall lined with columns that forms the garden's boundary.

THE ROMANTIC INDULGENCE
of a master landscape designer

AN EXQUISITE TRANQUILLITY PREVAILS IN THE STREETS AROUND THE BASILIQUE SAINTE-CLOTILDE, IN THE 7TH ARRONDISSEMENT. PRACTICALLY NO CARS, VERY LITTLE NOISE, JUST THE OCCASIONAL PASSER-BY AND CHILDREN PLAYING IN THE SQUARE – YOU COULD EASILY BELIEVE YOU WERE IN PROVINCIAL FRANCE.

This is a very privileged *quartier* with a number of secret gardens hidden away behind the somnolent façades. The garden featured here must be one of the most beautiful. It belongs to a superb eighteenth-century mansion, a family home par excellence.

An attractive paved inner courtyard leads to the garden at the back of the house. Its wonderfully balanced proportions and unusual design, the use of water, statues and architectural features of Renaissance inspiration, all help to create an atmosphere of great charm. Its shape is rectangular, with an oval pond in the middle of a broad lawn. Flagstones run round the perimeter. At the sides are two symmetrical raised terraces. Marble columns run alongside the back wall, and the handsome trees in the surrounding gardens make the space appear bigger than it is. The south-westerly orientation means the garden enjoys sun throughout the day. Our host tells us that this had been the home of his parents and grandparents. The morning light, he explains, makes the garden wonderfully alive, while at dusk it is flooded with a lovely soft glow.

'Our family moved here after the First World War. Both the buildings and the gardens had to be restored as they had suffered a lot of damage from Big Bertha, the huge German gun that bombarded Paris in the spring of 1918. Originally, there was nothing here but a vast expanse of grass. My grandparents had a liking for the theatre and enjoyed organizing performances for

their friends. The first thing they did was create raised areas at each end of the garden to form stages. The first performance was given in June 1921, with music by Reynaldo Hahn, and was directed by Colette's mime teacher. Our grandparents installed whatever embellishments they considered necessary. Having a penchant for antiquity, they imported the entire decor from Italy: columns, urns, vases. On the central axis of the façade, the oval pond was dug, which today is filled with water lilies and papyrus and also boasts a fountain. My grandmother loved flowers, especially roses, and planted lots of them.'

On the right-hand side of the garden, three steps lead up to a raised terrace, the entrance to which is marked by two eighteenth-century stone vases supported on low retaining walls. A honeysuckle with yellow corollas streaked with pink is trained over a simple wooden frame, forming a sort of windbreak. In direct line with the steps is a rocaille fountain, enveloped in a thick blanket of baby's tears (*Helxine soleirolii*) that the water has turned bright green. Its mossy texture and the light, bright appearance of the fountain accentuate the rococo feel. Emerging like an arrow from the left side of the green mass

Facing page, top: The house
opens directly on to
the peaceful garden.
The only sound is the splash
of the fountain.

Facing page, bottom: A rocaille
fountain flanked on the left
by a variegated *Ilex* and on
the right by the large leaves of
a *Gunnera.*

PICTURESQUE GARDENS

is a clump of dwarf bamboo, *Otatea acuminata*, with sharp pointed leaves. To the right, a *Gunnera* spreads its dark-green foliage, and a variegated ivy climbs the wall. The medley of greens is superb. To one side, the wall is covered with clematis; to the other, with roses. In the angle of the walls, two choisyas unfurl clouds of white flowers, framing a small stone bench where, if you sit for a moment, you are intoxicated by the fragrance of Mexican orange trees and lulled by the slap of water.

The choice of flowers reveals the discriminating eye of Louis Benech, who uses the simplest varieties and colour harmonies inspired by the work of Gertrude Jekyll, the famous English gardener of the early years of the twentieth century.

There are three dominant colours, blue, pink and white, set against a grey-green background of lavender, rosemary and santolinas. An array of irises – *Iris germanica*, *setosa* and *spuria* – runs the gamut of the blues: bright, dark, mauve, violet, purple. The pinks and whites are supplied by the honeysuckle, laburnums and old roses that climb over the walls. To either side of the central stone-rimmed pond stand two bushes covered in a profusion of small, delicate white flowers. These solid masses are big enough to lend a sense of depth but not so huge as to break up the space, which still seems open and unencumbered.

Along the wall with the colonnade, a similar unity prevails in the choice of species, with irises, hostas and a few clumps of ferns set against a background of climbing roses. A second terrace is situated at the opposite end of the garden to its counterpart, in an effect of harmonious symmetry. The French windows of one of the reception rooms open directly on to it, and it is a particularly pleasant spot to sit in the evenings because it catches the setting sun. A bust mounted on a stele is set above an eighteenth-century stone bench. A mass of pale-mauve clematis forms a cloak around it, spreading along the wall. The long, elegant house front provides the link between the two terraces. There is that indefinably attractive 'lived-in' look common to family houses, with the French windows left half-open and the shutters swinging loose.

The whole house speaks of ease, domestic happiness and a lack of pretension that have become rarities. The garden is full of life, with the children rushing outside at all hours of the day. They play together, chase one another, shriek with laughter. There is also the rare pleasure of being able to dine out of doors by the light of candles in glass shades.

Above: A border of *Iris germanica*, *setosa* and *spuria*.

HECTOR GUIMARD'S ART NOUVEAU GARDEN

A NUMBER OF PRIVATE HOUSES WERE BUILT NEAR THE PORTE D'AUTEUIL IN THE 16TH ARRONDISSEMENT DURING THE EARLY YEARS OF THE TWENTIETH CENTURY, OF WHICH SOME WERE DESIGNED BY ARCHITECTS INSPIRED BY ART NOUVEAU.

That was the case with the house we are visiting, which is half-hidden behind a curtain of vegetation, its porch submerged under a wonderful mauve wisteria that overflows on to the street. This was the first house built by Hector Guimard, who also designed the garden. The Art Nouveau style represented a conscious attempt to move away from the academic classicism which Guimard found quite unbearably ugly. He drew his inspiration from the flowing curves of plant forms, far better suited in his view to the realization of a true synthesis between architecture and decorative art. Guimard designed everything, both interiors and exteriors, with a sophistication sometimes bordering on mannerism.

As you pass through the gate, your eyes are drawn to the fantastical convolutions of the branches of a vast wisteria. A thick stand of bamboo to your left reinforces the sense of being surrounded by exuberant vegetation. The wisteria motif is one that crops up frequently in Art Nouveau decoration, being favoured because of its wonderful lilac colour and the oriental appearance of the interweaving branches. Also rather oriental in spirit is the typical Art Nouveau contrast between abundant vegetation and simple, clean-lined materials. Thus, the small path that leads through the garden is composed of pink bricks arranged on their edges in a herringbone pattern. The pleasure of walking through this riot of growth is enhanced by the contrast with its fine detailing and with the precision and artistry of the design.

Facing page: In front of the house, a path lined with bamboo plants, *Ilex* and clipped box leads to a small, sunny terrace.

Above: The entrance porch, overhung with mauve wisteria.

137

Another contrast is provided, when you recover from the first shock of the lush vegetation, by the discovery of the impeccable silhouettes of box globes, a variegated *Ilex* and a weeping dwarf conifer, its growth deliberately stunted by a process of hybridization. The effect here is similar to that of the dwarf species obtained by the Japanese art of bonsai.

Following the path, you find yourself face to face with a large bay window composed of the small leaded panes of glass beloved of Art Nouveau. The point of these was to minimize the transparency of the glass, which otherwise left the room too exposed, with the unvarying light that poured in from the front destroying all warmth or nuance and banishing any sense of intimacy. The glazing is enclosed in a wooden frame of dark-blue wood and there are tiled panels on either side representing climbing vines and yellow flowers, the blue centres of which echo the blue of the frame.

Next to the bay window, a wisteria climbs the wall of the house, mirroring the movement in the decorative panels. As you proceed towards the steps leading on to a small terrace, you pass a clipped choisya with its sentinel standard rose.

Facing page: The knotted stems
of a wisteria climb past
this magnificent Guimard
window with its flanking panels
of yellow tiling featuring
floral motifs.

Leaving behind the terrace and its neo-Gothic balustrade, you find yourself at the side of the house, the wall of which is covered with Virginia creeper (the vine leaf is another Art Nouveau motif). Bordering the alleyway is a perfectly cut bamboo hedge, at the foot of which Guimard positioned a slightly undulating line of white stones resting on their ends, which makes an unusual but interesting edging. This white line winds its way on into the garden, forming a boundary between the bushes and the lush green lawn. It has a very modern feel, somehow suggesting a blend of Antoni Gaudí, Jean Dubuffet and Niki de Saint Phalle. Where a straight stone border would dominate the planting, the motif incorporates the lawn and the bushes within the whole, giving the garden a contemporary sculptural look, a sense of being organic and alive.

Passing a number of pruned chestnut trees, you reach a large lawn from which the whole of the back of the house is visible, its generous bay windows overlooking a pink stone terrace. The façade is obscured at one point by a rounded mass of greenery, composed of a thicket of laurels and, set a little forward, a medlar with greeny-bronze lanceolate leaves. Planted below this are mahonias, hostas and fragrant geraniums with blue flowers.

On the terrace, hydrangeas are displayed in unusual planters made of slabs of slate pierced at the edges and fastened together. At the foot of the garden, a low studio is half-hidden behind a mass of choisyas, bamboo, lilac and rhododendrons. An ancient wisteria sprawls over the roof. In the shade of a magnolia, you can discern the elegant white flowers of *Hydrangea paniculata*.

Thanks to the dedication of its owners, Guimard's house has been restored to its former life and glory, with its once neglected gardens now setting it off to perfection.

Facing page: Bamboos form a tall screen behind the white wrought-iron bench.

Pages 144–45: A place for privacy in the garden, surrounded by lush vegetation.

A GREEN OASIS
in a secret setting

GARDENS ARE ESSENTIAL TO AUDE DE THUIN'S LIFE.
SHE HAS ONE IN CORSICA AND ONE IN PARIS. THEY ARE ALSO
CENTRAL TO HER PROFESSIONAL LIFE, AS SHE IS RESPONSIBLE
FOR THE HIGHLY SUCCESSFUL *L'ART DU JARDIN* SHOW HELD
IN PARIS EVERY YEAR IN THE MONTH OF JUNE.

Her Parisian garden in the 16th arrondissement is situated on a bend of the small road where she lives. As you open the hidden door in the exterior wall, which is crowned with the branches of lime trees, you have the impression of entering a secret garden.

You find yourself in shade. As shelter from the nearby houses, Aude de Thuin retained the original limes and added tall, leafy plants such as bamboo, which grows quickly and reaches a considerable height. To carry out the redesign of her small garden she chose Camille Muller, famous for his ability to create a magical atmosphere. His first step was to have everything dug over and large quantities of soil brought in. He then cut back the limes to create gaps for the light to penetrate.

Next, Muller divided the garden into two halves, the first adjacent to the house, which is a pleasant stone villa shrouded in greenery. This area remains quite heavily shaded, and here he installed a number of pot plants. The second area, however, was light enough to support a fine expanse of lawn, at the centre of which he placed a fountain. As you look back from

Facing page: Some details of the garden's décor are almost submerged by its rich vegetation.

here towards the house, you see a pretty conservatory, extended outwards by means of wooden decking. Here a table and chairs are discreetly dispersed among clumps of bamboo, globes of box in pots and giant-leaved gunneras, creating an alfresco salon. Looking up the garden from the central fountain, in the gap between the two masses of azaleas and rhododendrons that frame a wrought-iron fence, you see the entrance to the raised area. This section is designed as a winding path, bordered on either side with flowering shrubs, and leading towards the 'sheltered nook', a bamboo-fringed retreat containing a white wrought-iron bench and a gently perfumed choisya bush. Two impeccable balls of box in pots mark the entrance.

As you walk along the path, you have the pleasure of discovering clumps of day lilies and daisies, and also hellebores. At the very end of the garden is an enormous aviary which has no birds in it, only an unusual Venetian hanging ornament. On your way back to the house, which seems to nestle amid the greenery, your eye is drawn to a group of superb white tulips planted in pots.

Facing page: The box
elephant stands
impassively at the edge
of the 'jungle'.

PICTURESQUE GARDENS

AN ANIMAL PARADISE

THE OWNER OF THIS PROPERTY HAS A PASSION FOR GARDENING.
SHE LOVES THE WAY A GARDEN IS CONSTANTLY CHANGING,
AND IS NEVER HAPPIER THAN WHEN PRUNING AND PLANTING,
AND DISCOVERING NEW VARIETIES.

Wherever she lives, be it the Île-de-France or Haute-Provence, she leaves a garden behind her. In Paris, she agreed to lease a private mansion in the Faubourg Saint-Germain only on condition that she be allowed to create one at the back. Today it is one of the most original and most beautiful private gardens in the capital. The French windows of the salon open out on to a broad stone terrace, from which you have a view of the sizeable lawn bordered on either side with box hedges and framed by tall trees at the back.

Standing out against this screen of vegetation is an elephant of clipped box beside a clump of *Cotoneaster dammeri*, carefully chosen because in spring it attracts hordes of birds that love to eat the red berries. Behind the elephant is a stand of bamboo, *Pleioblastus viridistriatus*, which has yellow-green foliage, while four large clipped box spheres are ranged around the creature at a distance. Here, right in the heart of Paris, we have the spectacle of the elephant on the plains, standing at the forest's edge! It is a splendidly executed piece of sparkling originality.

Outside the French windows are earthenware pots planted with white tulips, a wonderfully fresh sight when you glimpse them from indoors. The same logic inspires the pots of *Clematis montana*, a plant more usually grown against the wall. Behind the box hedges at either side of the lawn are two shady gardens, reached by an attractively winding path. In spring, your progress

Facing page, top left: An inanimate tortoise basks in the sun.

Facing page, top right: *Clematis* 'Madame Lecoultre'.

Facing page, bottom left: Basket and secateurs are abandoned on the terrace by the owner as she makes a tour of her garden.

Facing page, bottom right: The stone elephant on the terrace echoes the theme of the topiary.

is accompanied by the fragrance of the white-flowering narcissi, hellebores and hostas that spring up from the attractive ground cover of *Lamium* and *Ajuga reptans*.

Clinging to the trellis-covered walls, as well as many of the trees, are old varieties of rose that light up the undergrowth, among them 'Perle d'Or', a China rose 'Bobbie James', which is white, and 'Aloha'. In the background is honeysuckle, *Lonicera* 'Halliana', and *Clematis* 'Madame Lecoultre', wrapped around a tree. There is a splendid contrast between the central garden, which is clipped, bare and dark green, and the teeming growth at the sides, with sometimes hundreds of roses clustering on a single tree.

Among the undergrowth the owner has introduced subtle accents of *Mahonia japonica*, which turns bronze in the autumn and bears scented flowers in winter, and, a little further on, a yellow-flowering jasmine that retains its fragrance through the winter. At the foot of the garden, you can walk through the undergrowth to a small green 'room' of topiaried ivy. There you can sit down peacefully on a wrought-iron bench and succumb to the intoxicating perfume of a magnificent syringa, *Philadelphus* 'Virginal'.

A great plant lover, the owner likes original ideas that keep her enthusiasm high. She has, for example, retained a big elderberry as an ornamental tree, just because she is so fond of the bunches of purply-black berries that are such a magnet for the blackbirds.

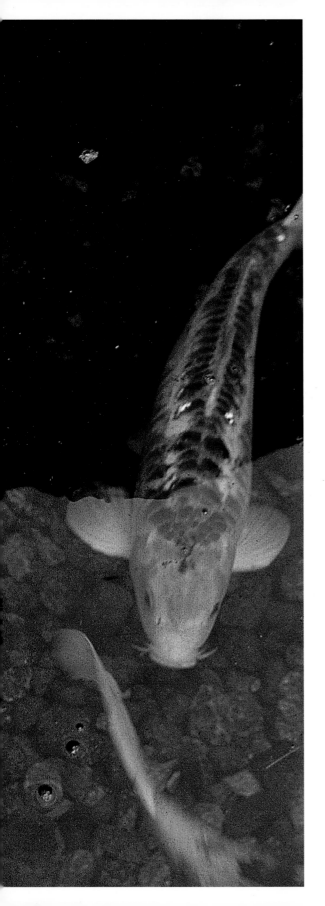

EXOTIC
GARDENS

A TASTE OF RURAL RUSSIA
at Baron and Baronne d'Orgeval's *isba*

HOW TIMES CHANGE! IN THE THIRTEENTH CENTURY,
KING PHILIPPE AUGUSTE SAW THE NEED TO ENCLOSE HIS BELOVED
CITY OF PARIS WITHIN PROTECTIVE WALLS, WHILE UNDER
THE SECOND EMPIRE (1852 – 70), THE FINANCIER BARON PEREIRE
WAS CONVINCED THAT WHAT THE PEOPLE OF PARIS NEEDED
ABOVE ALL WAS INCREASED FREEDOM OF MOVEMENT.
AS A RESULT HE BUILT THE AUTEUIL RAILWAY, FOLLOWING THE ROUTE
OF AN ANCIENT TRACK SKIRTING THE BOIS DE BOULOGNE.

Above: The *isba* was formerly part of the Imperial Russian pavilion at the Paris Exposition held in 1867.

Facing page: Old roses are trained over the façade of the *isba*, providing a cascade of exquisite blooms.

He was a man who took a great interest in architecture; indeed, he conceived such a passion for the Imperial Russian pavilion on display at the Paris Exposition of 1867 that, when the exhibition was over, he had the part of the pavilion he wished to preserve, the *isba*, transported to a new site near La Muette, in the west of the city.

In the eighteenth century, people used to embellish their estates with follies and pagodas, allowing them to contemplate examples of the achievements of different civilizations. It was very much in that spirit that the *isba* was installed in the former Parc de Beauséjour, now occupied in part by the Jardin du Ranelagh. Today, the *isba* is the home of the Baron and Baronne d'Orgeval.

The house reflects its rustic origins, with timber walls and roof ornamented with a perforated wooden trim. The interior is decorated in the neoclassical style favoured in the palaces of St Petersburg. It is this typically Russian

Facing page: Beside the French windows leading into the salon, more magnificent roses bloom.

Pages 158–59: 'Cunningham's White' rhododendrons in Florentine pots stand on either side of the front door, which is constructed of Russian timber with a blond burr finish.

contrast between the natural and the sophisticated that the d'Orgevals wanted to accentuate by creating a garden that would set off the building like a jewel.

'When I acquired the *isba* some twenty-five years ago,' the Baron recalls, 'where the garden now stands there were stables in a very bad state of repair. I had everything demolished so that I could plant a garden of perennials, because I love their wild appearance, although I took care to choose some of the more interesting species: wood anemones, hellebores, pelargoniums, shadberries.' In accordance with his plan, the Baron d'Orgeval planted flowering shrubs rarely seen in Parisian gardens, along with camellias, photinias, *Ceanothus impressus* and hydrangeas. One of these is *H. arborescens quercifolia* 'Snow Queen', which has off-white panicles flecked with pink, and generous leaves that turn red in the course of the season, harmonizing well with the golden tints of autumn.

'I also like rhododendrons,' he explains, 'because they form big bushes with very delicate flowers, in particular R. "Cunningham's White", which I've put in Florentine pots by the front door. To ensure the house maintains its rustic charm, I take care that there are always flowers about: in winter, snowdrops, camellias and hellebores; in spring, old roses which I allow to run wild and grow into bushes; in summer, mahonias and hydrangeas, which stay in flower until the first frosts. The house is an exceptional relic of the past, and by ensuring that it is maintained in close proximity to nature, I feel that I've prevented it from being turned into a museum.

'When I am in the garden, I am always staggered by the architecture, and I sometimes catch myself wondering if I am not a million miles away from Paris.'

Facing page: The eighteenth-century sphinx crouches amid the foliage, a silently questioning presence.

Pages 162–63: The house is almost hidden by the lush vegetation in the courtyard.

AN ITALIAN FANTASY
in a Parisian courtyard

HALF COURTYARD, HALF GARDEN, THIS PLACE OWES ITS CHARM
TO THE UNUSUAL BLEND OF TWO STYLES. IN DESIGN, IT IS A COURTYARD,
AND YET IT HAS ALL THE APPEAL OF A GARDEN.

It is under the spell of the sphinx who inhabits it, crouched amid the foliage, surveying all around with her stony gaze. At first, as you pass through the porchway, you see before you nothing but a perfectly ordinary courtyard. Only as you advance do you become aware of the silence that casts a pall over everything. Here the greenery impregnates its surroundings and imposes its own rhythms, in an atmosphere of cool shade and meditative peace with which all lovers of the forest will be familiar. You think you have fallen through time, that you are living in a dream. And you are right. This is a fantasy world you are inhabiting, for the reality is that you are on the Right Bank in the very heart of Paris. With its neglected air and riotous vegetation, typical of old Italian gardens, the scene before you derives its charm from the fact that it is a poetic evocation of passing time. The sphinx's face is slightly worn, green mosses have invaded her stone plinth. The grass grows wild along walls hung with stray strands of Virginia creeper. Ferns proliferate, flourishing in the humidity that always seems to prevail when nature is left to its own devices.

And yet, the air of neglect is a sham, for this garden represents in fact the height of luxury. The abundance of the vegetation is all the more alluring for being the product of a perfectly controlled environment. The gravel, for example, is beautifully raked and the rampant ivy regularly cut back. Disorder appeals here precisely because it conceals perfect order.

You are reluctant to leave such a magical spot, which paradoxically combines a hint of Italian nostalgia with an insouciance that is pure eighteenth-century France.

KENZO'S MINIATURE JAPANESE LANDSCAPE

THE COUTURIER KENZO IS FAMOUS FOR HIS ZEST FOR LIFE.

His fashions are vibrant combinations of a number of popular folk traditions, inspired by a view of the world in which nature plays a central part. His dresses resemble the flowers he loves. Kenzo has lived in Paris for many years and could not imagine an existence in a house without a garden. 'I have an urgent need to be in close and permanent contact with nature. For me it is a source of inspiration, because of its colours and constant changes. It brings me tranquillity.'

Having already owned several houses and gardens in Paris, this time Kenzo wanted his new home to have a Japanese garden. His search led him to a former factory with a piece of land adjacent to it, in a street near the Place de la Bastille (east of the Marais). 'I called on the services of Iwaku, who is a famous landscape designer in Japan, and asked him to create an authentically Japanese garden with a river, a waterfall, carp, stones brought back from my country and typically Japanese flora: bamboo, pines, cherry trees, maples. My idea was that I should be able both to look out at the garden from the house and also to live in it, using the terrace for breakfast and dinner and for strolling about.' The works were so extensive that they took five years to complete, and Kenzo had to move into the house before the garden was quite finished. Iwaku imported vast quantities of soil and had to resolve complicated problems involving the water supply before he could install the pines, camellias, maples, cherries and bamboo.

Facing page, top:
Kenzo's house, framed by
the red of a Japanese maple
and the yellowish-green of a
stand of bamboo *Phyllostachys
pubescens.*

Facing page, bottom left:
In springtime, the cherry
tree covers the terrace in
a shower of blossom.

Facing page, bottom right:
The pool is stocked with
koi carp.

'I wanted a garden that would be a sort of landscape in miniature, planned in precise detail but retaining a natural appearance. That is why I ask Iwaku to come back once a year to work on it and ensure the trees and plants still create that effect. The salon opens on to the garden, as do my bedroom and the Japanese bathroom. So I can contemplate this wonderful "landscape" everywhere I go.' Kenzo decorated the house himself in an eclectic style combining old Japanese furniture, Louis XV armchairs and contemporary objets d'art.

The garden is an ideal place for meditation and creative inspiration: 'Bamboo, roses, irises all stimulate my imagination with their beauty and simplicity.' Kenzo also enjoys watching the changing seasons. 'I particularly enjoy early spring when the buds appear on the spreading branches of the big cherry tree, and the autumn when the maple turns red. I also like planting pots of peonies, irises and chrysanthemums, and absorbing myself in the contemplation of my carp as they glide through the water.'

Kenzo can claim to have found a way of living in Japan without stirring from the heart of Paris.

Below: Delicate maple foliage mingles with graceful ferns.

Facing page: The exquisitely interlaced foliage of maples and giant tree-ferns.

Pages 172–73: The cascading foliage of weeping willow, maples and bamboos is massed together with *Gunnera*, ferns, baby's tears (*Helxine soleirolii*) and much more to give this garden its luxuriant appearance.

A LUSH ASIAN PARADISE
on the Left Bank

THE LEFT BANK STILL BOASTS A FEW BROAD, SHADY AVENUES WHERE AN ATMOSPHERE OF TRANQUILLITY PREVAILS, A REMINDER OF A BUCOLIC PAST. THE PRIVATE GARDENS HIDDEN AWAY BEHIND THEIR NINETEENTH-CENTURY FAÇADES ARE TESTAMENT TO THE FACT THAT ONLY A SHORT TIME AGO THIS AREA WAS STILL COUNTRYSIDE.

One of these gardens is exceptional, a triumph of inspiration and hard work, and a shining example of what can be achieved between an enlightened amateur and a landscape designer, in this case Robert Bazelaire. Passing through the apartment that opens directly on to the garden, the vision that greets you through the French windows is dazzling. There before you, in the centre of Paris, is an exotic garden of subtropical luxuriance, a scene of oriental enchantment.

All that was here originally was an unremarkable garden, composed mainly of a lawn and a few hardy perennials. The woman who owns the apartment is Indian, and she determined to create a garden that would be a reminder, in some sense, of the continent where she was born.

What is so extraordinary is the way you are plunged suddenly into another world. The rich greens and blues, the astonishingly soft light filtering through the trees, the perfection of the ground cover, together they create an atmosphere of such exquisite delicacy that you feel this is a haven, a place where you are safe and enclosed.

The lushness of the vegetation comes from the southern exposure and the protection of walls clad with Virginia creeper, reinforced in places by stands of tall bamboo. The walls effectively shelter the garden from wind and cold, but they do not block out the strong midday sun, making this spot a cocoon of warmth and light. There are no straight lines or sharp angles here, the unity of the ensemble being built up of gentle curves and gradations. In front of the house, a Japanese medlar casts a gentle shade. Amid an expanse of bright

Facing page, top left: A stream winds through luxuriant vegetation.

Facing page, top right: The bust of a Buddha posed beneath a tree fern lends a reverent aura to this verdant garden.

Facing page, bottom left: Primulas, crocuses and royal-blue *Iris japonica* are grouped to picturesque effect around a green-tinged rock.

green, a weeping willow stands by a pretty stream edged with tall grasses. In the middle of the garden, a clump of *Cornus* and tree peonies marks the spot where the paths diverge and lead on to another semi-enclosed garden. Here, the smooth mat of green underfoot resembles a lake. It is fringed with tropical ferns, with stepping stones placed at intervals to encourage you to pause and contemplate the nearby plants.

There are many forking paths, many choices, and every time you walk in the garden you stumble on previously unexplored areas. The number of species is restricted, but within each species there are many varieties. The bamboos take up relatively little space, yet they give the impression of a jungle because there are something like twenty-five varieties growing here. The bulbous forms of *Arundinaria viridistriata* contrast with the black canes and mauve shadows of *Phyllostachys nigra*. The same holds true for the tropical ferns and the maples.

This is a connoisseur's garden. Many subtle touches go into creating the impression of luxuriance. A similar care has been taken in selecting interesting and unusual foliage. The medlar has finely demarcated, elongated leaves, the willow has narrow leaves like ribbons. The foliage of the maples resembles lightly falling rain, echoing the form of the fern fronds. The overall effect of the foliage is to soften the light, creating enchanting effects and variations.

This is a seasonal garden, with the passage of time reflected in its changing colours. In winter, the scene is lit up by the white and yellow of snowdrops, hellebores, heathers and crocuses. A month later come the blues that herald the spring, with irises, violets, scented hyacinths and primulas. Autumn brings a glow of reds and yellows.

You are greeted by a variety of sensations. At first you hear just the faint splash of water, which gradually becomes a gentle flow, and then a distinct babble. Like the water, the wind rushing through the bamboos wafts perfume towards you, a fragrant mixture of gardenias, tuberoses and jasmines. Distinctively shaped rocks stand dotted about the garden, like human presences. There is a headless statue of a Buddha. The garden comfortably embraces all these diverse influences.

AFRICAN AND ORIENTAL INFLUENCES

IN THIS *QUARTIER* OF THE 7TH ARRONDISSEMENT,
A NUMBER OF GARDENS HAVE BEEN CREATED OUT OF LAND
FORMERLY OCCUPIED BY OLD CRAFT WORKSHOPS.

As the businesses collapsed, so the workshops were gradually replaced by gardens – very much at a premium in this area. That was how the garden we are concerned with here came into being. Originally it was no more than a small courtyard surrounded by a number of houses on different levels, which had been used in the late nineteenth century for the manufacture of ceramics.

When the new owner took possession, he decided to retain some of the buildings to convert into a house, and to preserve the differences of level. His plan was to make these into terraces, looking down on to the garden situated in the central courtyard area. The idea of an exotic garden, and in particular one with an oriental feel, came from the discovery of walls of fine blue ceramic. In collaboration with architect Paul Nataf and landscape designer Michel Boulcour, the decision was taken to divide the garden into three levels. The top level was conceived as a semi-arid area, and featured an African hut; the second as a bog garden, with an enormous rock and a spring; and the third as a space filled with light, a bright, sunny garden near the house, planted with white flowers. 'When I moved in,' the owner recalls, 'I remembered a visit I made as a child to George Sand's house in Nohant, and a rather splendid cabin that looked like an African hut, made of logs arranged in an attractive grid pattern, with a straw roof. I wanted to do something similar and put it in the corner by the

Facing page: In the bog garden, a mauve-flowering hydrangea contrasts with the ferns and arum lilies growing around the base of the grotto.

wall as part of the semi-arid area.' A climbing hydrangea covers the whole of the back wall.

A few stone steps lead down into the bog garden. There the owner had the original idea of installing a huge rock brought back from Saint-Jean-de-Beauregard (about twenty miles south of Paris). Positioned on stone blocks set on their sides, the rock forms a sort of grotto. From the spring inside, water flows in a pretty, winding rivulet. Above the rock stand clipped spheres of box and a group of *Hydrangea aspera* 'Villosa', with flat-headed mauve flowers. More box spheres surround the foot of the rock, as well as hostas with leaves as large as lily pads, bluey-green in colour, clumps of ferns and quantities of arum lilies, whose pure, glowing white corollas light up the grotto. The pale-green foliage of a quince overhangs the rock in elegant fashion. Beautiful *Iris japonica* of an intense blue illuminate the dark background, as does the bright clematis that clings to the rock in the company of scattered clumps of day lilies.

Facing page: The elegant garden on the lower terrace, suffused with light.

Below, left: Ferns, arum lilies and hostas thrive in the shade of the grotto, flanked by clipped balls of box.

Below, right: A twisting spiral staircase blends into the setting like a climbing plant.

More globes of box terminate the second level and open the sweep of the third terrace. Here, clumps of white-flowering hostas are set against the off-white of the gravel. A table and a few chairs make this sunny garden a pleasant spot for lunch or dinner, which you can reach through the French windows. Perhaps a quarter of the terrace is shaded by the branches of a tall lime tree. The climbing rose *Rosa* 'Kiftsgate' is trained against the wall, its abundance of white flowers in harmony with the generally luxuriant air of the whole garden. A *Cornus* with attractive pale-green foliage, ravishing white peonies and a few hydrangeas provide the elegant finishing touches for the ground-level garden. A spiral staircase leads up to a small terrace on the first storey, from which you can look down and survey the ensemble. The balustrade and parapet are hung with ivy, and pots of pink and white single-flowered camellias sit out in the sun.

The owner used to enjoy holding parties outside. At Christmas, the whole garden would be decorated with coloured balls, to the vast delight of the children. At Easter, they loved to search for presents hidden behind the box trees or deep inside the grotto. In spring, during the long evenings lit by candlelight, the garden takes on a fairytale aspect.

The property has since changed hands, but the new owners have retained the unusual structure. They are collectors of contemporary art and have added their own touch of originality by erecting a bronze statue of a giant near the spiral staircase. Two antique lions flank the door to the garden, which remains the focus of the whole house.

A SPIRITUAL HAVEN

THE FASHION DESIGNER RENATA WANTED A HOUSE
WITH A GARDEN, BOTH AS A PLACE TO LIVE WITH HER FAMILY
AND AS A LOCATION FOR A WORKSHOP TO DEVELOP
HER FABULOUS COLLECTIONS OF SILK DRESSES.

Between Montparnasse and Saint-Germain, she found exactly what she was looking for, a charmingly provincial retreat tucked away in a quiet street near the Rue de Rennes. The prospect of living in this comfortable house dating from the early years of the twentieth century was immediately attractive, but the garden too played its part in the decision, being an indispensable element of the lifestyle she envisaged.

'For me,' explains Renata, 'a garden is a place for quiet meditation as well as enjoyment. So I was thrilled to learn that back in the eighteenth century there was a Carmelite convent on the site! I do believe that creating a garden has a certain spiritual dimension. The love of plants and the link with nature, those are two things that now I couldn't manage without.

'When we moved in, there was just an overgrown plot of land, covered in ivy and gravel: a disaster. I had the impression no one had really loved it. But it was of a decent size and the south-facing exposure was a plus. Over the wall, a magnificent hundred-year-old plane tree dominated the garden, providing shade over a good quarter of the plot.

Facing page: The garden, seen through the French windows of the salon.

Above: Palm trees at the foot of the pergola.

Facing page, top: The yellow
of the roses blooming on the
pergola is echoed by clusters of
fruit growing on the palms.

Facing page, bottom right:
Figures of cherubs peer
out from the black canes
of a clump of bamboo,
Phyllostachys nigra.

'Half shade, half sun, it captured my imagination and I could see all sorts
of intriguing possibilities. My husband and I fell in love with it because we
thought it was so right for us. You should know that I am German and my
husband is Mediterranean. My sister, Ulricke Klages, is an agronomist and
landscape designer, and she took this north–south axis as her starting point.
There is sun from eleven in the morning to eight in the evening during the
finest part of the year. In the sunny area, we planted palm trees, yuccas, a
hibiscus, a white wisteria, a camellia (also white) and near it a magnolia.
We had a pergola built, with roses climbing over it. It's an absolute delight.
When we're in the house, we love looking out at the garden.'

Klages added volume and depth by introducing low mounds of soil planted
with rhododendron bushes, with a path winding through them. This raised
area is set at a diagonal and gives the whole garden a dynamism it previously
lacked as a static, flat expanse.

In the shady area, clumps of rhododendrons, fragrant geraniums and impatiens introduce patches of colour. There is also a corner planted with ferns and
bamboo, *Phyllostachys nigra*, which has wonderful black canes and elegant
broken foliage. A lovely mauve wisteria and white roses climb over the back
wall of the house. Palm trees mask the far corner. Beyond the terrace extends
a carpet of baby's tears (*Helxine soleirolii*), introducing a softer, fresher feeling.

You could easily imagine it is a pond covered in duckweed. The trunks of yuccas rise out of the green expanse. 'It is here we put out our chairs and loungers, this is where we relax and read and have tea. To make the garden even more an extension of the house, we opened up one of the walls and built a patio. This blurs the distinction between indoors and outdoors; it makes the garden part of the house. The garden is also integrated with my work space. On my sister's advice, we arranged things so that it provides the link between the house and the studio. My professional life isn't cut off from my private life, nor indeed from my garden, which can sometimes be a source of inspiration.'

When she walks to work through her garden, Renata always pauses to do some watering or pull up a few weeds. 'Sometimes I linger for an hour, more or less *en passant*', she says. 'My husband used to know nothing about plants and couldn't make anything grow, but now he has become a keen amateur gardener. He looks after the plants and uses biological insecticides so as not to harm the birds. As it isn't as cold in Paris during the winter as outside the city, we have tits and robins seeking sanctuary with us. Hearing a blackbird sing for us in the spring, seeing the camellias flower at Christmas, and the roses in bloom for most of the year – some don't disappear until the first frosts of January – all those things add another dimension to our life as city-dwellers.'

Index of landscape gardeners and property owners

Acknowledgements

Thank you to all those people who welcomed us into their gardens, and to everyone who contributed to the publication of this book.